THE LIFE SCIENCE ENTREPRENEUR

THE LIFE SCIENCE ENTREPRENEUR

A PRACTICAL GUIDE TO FORMING, FINANCING, BUILDING, AND EXITING A LIFE SCIENCE COMPANY

Jack J. Luchese

ISBN: 1533483957
ISBN 13: 9781533483959
Library of Congress Control Number: 2016909201
CreateSpace Independent Publishing Platform
North Charleston, South Carolina

TABLE OF CONTENTS

Introduction · ix

Chapter 1   The Initial Planning Phase · 1

The Compelling Idea · 1

Understanding Strategic Market Demand · · · · · · · · · 4

Chapter 2   The Start-Up Phase· 9

The Importance of Strong Intellectual Property· · · · · 9

Forming a Legal Entity for Your Start-Up Company · · · 13

Articulating Your Long-Term Business Strategy · · · · 15

Chapter 3   Initial Formation of the Business · · · · · · · · · · · · · · · · 20

Company Form Determination · · · · · · · · · · · · · · · · 20

Board of Directors Formation · · · · · · · · · · · · · · · · 21

Board Committee Formation and Purpose· · · · · · · · 26

Chapter 4   Funding / Capital Formation ·34

                The Management Factor in Fundraising · · · · · · · ·34

                Preparing Your Company for Fundraising · · · · · · · ·36

                Founder's Stage ·39

                Seed Stage ·40

                Special Funding Programs · · · · · · · · · · · · · · · · · ·40

                Angel Financing ·41

                Venture Financing ·42

                Institutional Financing ·46

                Mezzanine Financing ·46

                The IPO and the Role of the Lead Underwriter · · · ·47

                Secondary Public Offering of Shares · · · · · · · · · · ·52

Chapter 5   Organizational Development ·55

                Operational Resources ·55

                Developing Your Product/Idea · · · · · · · · · · · · · · ·56

                Managing Your Cash and Budget· · · · · · · · · · · · · ·59

                Developing Your Strategic Plan · · · · · · · · · · · · · ·60

                Investor Relations ·64

Chapter 6   Building Your Executive Team · · · · · · · · · · · · · · · · · · 66

            What is the Normal Source of the CEO Talent Pool? · · 67

            Human Resource Planning · · · · · · · · · · · · · · · · · · · 70

            Finance and Accounting · 76

            Operations/Manufacturing · · · · · · · · · · · · · · · · · · 77

            Sales and Marketing · 79

            Business Development · 83

            Research and Development · · · · · · · · · · · · · · · · · · 84

            Intellectual Property Enhancements · · · · · · · · · · · 93

Chapter 7   Establishing Strategic Goals and Objectives · · · · · · · · · 95

            Embracing the Culture of Business Planning · · · · · · 97

            The Thousand-Day Plan · · · · · · · · · · · · · · · · · · · 99

Chapter 8   Managing Operational Effectiveness · · · · · · · · · · · · · 103

            Management Effectiveness · · · · · · · · · · · · · · · · · · 106

            Matrix Management · 112

Chapter 9   Compensation · 116

            Board / Board Committee Level · · · · · · · · · · · · · · 116

            Executive Management Team · · · · · · · · · · · · · · · 118

Non Executive Management · · · · · · · · · · · · · · · · · 119

Non Management Employees · · · · · · · · · · · · · · · · 119

Overall Considerations · 120

Chapter 10 The Commercialization Phase · · · · · · · · · · · · · · · 122

Partnering/Licensing Pathway · · · · · · · · · · · · · · 122

Product/Service Sales Pathway · · · · · · · · · · · · · · 133

Chapter 11 Value Creation · 144

Understanding What and How Value is Created · · · 144

Concept of Present Value Analysis · · · · · · · · · · · · 146

Value Creation by Type of Business Strategy · · · · · · 149

1. For a Development Company · · · · · · · · · · · · 149

2. For a Fully-Integrated Operating Company · · 151

Chapter 12 The Exit Phase · 157

Preparing Your Due Diligence Package · · · · · · · · · 157

Value Determination · 158

Chapter 13 Conclusion · 183

Acknowledgments · 189

INTRODUCTION

I f you purchased this book, most likely you have a great idea and wish to turn it into a great commercial success. This book is a general, practical guide to anyone thinking of starting a company in the life sciences industry or anyone that would like a general overview of what is involved in this business. The life sciences industry in this case is defined as traditional pharmaceuticals, biotech, biological products, imaging, medical devices, diagnostics, and drug-delivery technologies, all of which involve the following:

- High-value, educated, skilled human resources
- Strong intellectual property rights
- Long product-gestation periods, as much as ten years
- Well-developed regulation at the federal and state levels
- Raising large amounts of capital to both develop and commercialize a product

My years in the industry have provided me the opportunity to experience many things first hand. The experience has been wonderful; I've worked with Big Pharma for about half my career and small emerging companies for the other half. Understanding the perspective of both of these cultures has benefited me enormously when I've attempted to conduct business between the groups.

As you read this book imagine that *you* are the CEO on the cover of this book. The random cover image used is meant to convey a confident, middle aged, committed, serious, intelligent individual ready to be the CEO of a start-up company. Rather than being a how-to book, this book is a practical guide written by someone who has lived through the process of taking companies from start-up to exit and can speak from the point of view of actually having done all this. In addition, the book is more of a conversation between one CEO that has experienced this process and you, perhaps a new CEO just beginning this process. Alternatively, you may be someone that has a desire to know more about the life sciences industry from a start-up perspective. In reading this book, consider me a counselor that can help you to define your ultimate objective and to stay focused on that objective during this long journey. As you read, you will learn more about the development and regulatory process, the commercialization sequence, and the importance of a good plan and a high-quality management team. Finally, you will learn about the very important need to plan for and develop quality, committed funding sources to allow you to execute your plan. Success requires the simultaneous management of many disciplines contributing to a successful business objective using capital and driven by quality professionals. You are the maestro of this orchestra, and this book is your practical guide.

During my career I have had the opportunity to work in business development, new products, field sales, and accounting, domestic and international business models, before moving into general management. All my participation in product launches, manufacturing design and start-ups, company formations, acquisitions, mergers, divestitures, capital formation, downsizing, upsizing for growth, clinical trials, and regulatory challenges provided me a rich learning experience. As a CEO I had the opportunity to manage a small publicly traded company and a large private international company. I directed downsizing programs, restructurings, and the formation of several new subsidiaries; launched a major biotech product worldwide; raised capital in numerous private and public transactions; and executed mergers and key partnering deals with Big Pharma and small biotech companies. My experiences involved companies ranging in employee size from 5 to 2,500 employees and from zero to hundreds of millions of dollars in sales. My journey was broad in scope, involving products in pharmaceuticals, biotech, biologics, medical devices, and consumer products. All of my experiences afforded to me the opportunity to participate in and observe activities from many points of view. Along this journey I also learned what failure and success look like. None of this makes me smarter than anyone else; it just gave me the opportunity to describe to you what I learned and observed so that you can make your own judgment on how to proceed.

One of the things you will quickly realize in starting a new company and/or being the chief executive of a company is that on occasion it can be lonely at the top. There are times when it is not practical or appropriate to discuss many things with your immediate staff and/or employees in general. You may express your enthusiasm, but it is good to have someone to confide in and seek counsel from. As you run your own business and make key decisions, just remember that the decisions you make in the beginning will impact you throughout the life of the company. Therefore, be thoughtful, not emotional, when making critical strategic decisions, and think of the steps that follow that might be impacted by the decision you are about to make. For best results, never lose sight of the long-term business objective, and keep your eyes and ears on the near-term activities that will get you to your intended end point.

In a small start-up company, the CEO (chief executive officer) and the management team that the CEO recruits for his/her executive team are the key to success. What you do and how you do it matters at every stage of the development of your business. Read on.

CHAPTER 1

THE INITIAL PLANNING PHASE

Ready, aim, fire—in that order!

The Compelling Idea

The world still loves a great idea! One of the most important things to remember when forming a business is that you must offer something new and special to the marketplace. Sameness is not sexy, nor does it attract capital, the best management talent, or the best advisors and board members.

The "better mousetrap" concept is always useful to consider when deciding upon any business venture. The life sciences business relies on technology, capital, and highly skilled talent to succeed. The newer, better idea or technology draws a crowd, and the other ideas usually struggle and have to settle for less. However, it is the truly disruptive technologies that often get the most attention and capital.

The word *disruptive* is often misused to mean anything that presents a positive change or better idea. On the contrary, a disruptive technology is a market/business-model game changer that is generally unexpected. Its introduction strategically and materially impacts the current use of products, service providers, distribution channels, and pricing. This creates a situation that is certainly unwanted by established competitive players in the current market. Truly disruptive technologies are few and far between, and they represent the Holy Grail sought by every entrepreneur. If you have one, you will know it because the world will beat a path to your doorway; if you have to convince everyone you meet that your idea is disruptive, it probably is not. Some examples that we all know of include the Internet, e-mail, the iPhone, Amazon.com, and Facebook. Be careful to wisely and appropriately use the word "disruptive" in your communications so as not to lose credibility with your audience.

You are about to begin a long journey during which you eventually will commit enormous amounts of energy, opportunity time, and personal financial capital. Make sure it is the best idea you can come up with and that it has strong market acceptance and feasibility before you make such an enormous commitment of yourself. You may have a fantastic strategic money making idea that you should pursue. However, before you charge into this venture make sure you have a plan and the financing secured to carry you through the first set of milestones. Sometimes you get anxious and feel the need to make it happen, and you charge because you are ready to charge, not because you should. There is nothing wrong with allowing yourself to let your thinking mature on this important matter, gather some more thoughts, resources, capital sources, intelligence, and some additional ideas, and then make the commitment, as you will then be better prepared.

I am going to ask you to think backward this one time; that is, before you start a company, think about how you are going to exit that business some day. The exit strategy should be clear, and you should always create a situation whereby you have multiple exit options, not just one, because you need to be open to varying exit transaction types. Think in terms of five to ten years, not one to two years, unless the business model / idea you are considering happens to be a two-year business venture by definition. Competition in the form of new technologies and new talent is all around us, so you need to invest your resources in a business that has staying power for all the future steps necessary to grow it and finally to exit it. The start-up and growth phases of the business are exciting, but in the end it is the exit that will make the difference for you and your family, so keep your eye on the exit strategy at all times. Your future investors will also be thinking strategically, so make it easy for them to invest by articulating the possible exit strategies. Most of them already know what these strategies are, but they want to hear it from you to make sure you have one.

I cannot overemphasize the importance of selecting a truly exceptional idea to build your business. However, for that idea to develop into a successful business investment, it must be all of these things:

- Favorably positioned
- Protected by patents and/or trade secrets
- Feasible to develop and commercialize
- Financed by patient third-party investment sources
- Designed to meet the specific needs of a target market that will readily embrace it

The compelling idea can come in many forms. It could be a biomedical discovery that shows a compelling therapeutic pathway to a cure for a major disease. It could be a new system of distribution to a new sales channel or to all existing channels. Or it could be the merging of several great product concepts into one business model that brings synergy and can command a premium price in the marketplace, to name a few. This compelling idea is something you will present thousands of times to customers, employees, investors, agencies, and service providers. Celebrate your idea, simplify it, communicate it, and make it part of everything you do going forward. Yes, of course you will develop new ideas, but it is imperative that your first idea succeeds, because you may not get a chance to fund a second one.

Now for a dose of hard reality. Building a company from scratch and turning it into a success—that is, a profitable business—is very difficult to do. You must be firmly committed to doing it, and you need to be realistic about how it will impact you personally. First of all, it will be exciting and give you a great rush. You will feel good about yourself and think you are somebody special. You first need that level of confidence

3

in yourself. This journey will require you to work harder than you have ever worked before. You will be excited about the opportunities for success. At the same time, you will worry about cash, the things that can go wrong, and anticipate that people will doubt you and your business plan. My father often said, "There is no record of anyone drowning from sweat." That may be true, but there will be times when all this will feel like waterboarding. You will have to have thick skin, your personal finances will be strained to the limit, your fun in life will become building your business, and you will be obsessed with every achievement, opportunity, and setback. You will worry that you missed something and that another CEO on the other side of town, or the world, is developing a better idea for the same target market. Finally, you will have to temper your enthusiasm and emotions to launch this effort only when the time is right and the cash and other resources are lined up in your favor. If you launch too soon and commit to too many resources before you are ready to fund them, you run the risk of a company stall, and a stall will hurt you in the long run. Now if you are ready for this, then go for it and read on. Welcome to the world of a life sciences entrepreneur.

Understanding Strategic Market Demand

Someone once said, you only need a customer to start a business. This timeless statement remains true. Clearly this principle is a little easier to appreciate when applied to a retail business or a service business where the gestation period from idea to launch to customers is a year or two. It is also true for a technology business, but we all know it takes many expensive steps to get there, so it is a much longer road to satisfying that first customer. It is imperative that you are crystal clear about the likelihood of the market accepting your new idea/product, and it is important that you convince others first of this hypothesis and then prove to future investors that your conclusion is absolutely correct.

Often target markets and product/service sales projections are lumped together in a single conversation. To enable all third parties to have the same confidence you have in your market and sales projections, it is useful to be prepared to walk them through the process one

4

component at a time. Conference rooms are loaded with slide presenta-tions that show fancy charts showing sales of a certain product category rising into the billions of dollars worldwide over time. Everybody has seen these charts, so you don't need to show more macro data on a broad market category. Frankly, I have never found these simplistic charts to be all that useful except to make an initial point of macro market potential. Very often what is more convincing to a third-party viewer is a market presentation that first analyzes the several specific segments that drive the broad macro market over time, followed by a further analysis of the specific market segment you plan to target and launch in to build mar-ket share over time.

All markets are dynamic. They are typically a collection of customer and product classes, often referred to as market segments. It is important to understand every market in terms of both units and dollars. Knowing the interaction of unit market share (and the various prices by segment) is what eventually develops into a quality, informed, dollar market forecast. These segments uniquely define a market and are in a state of continuous change. The percentage of the total market comprising a given segment changes over time, as do the product-category percentages within the seg-ment. Market forecasting should be dynamic, and your assessment of the growth of the strategic market should reflect a thoughtful analysis of what segments are growing and shrinking over time. A quality strategic sales fore-cast is built upon a good base of strategic market-segment forecasts. Some market segments may include the following:

Market Segments by Customer Class

Customer class could mean domestic or international; it could mean private sector or government (federal, state, local, military, Veterans Administration); it could also mean pediatrics, hospital based, seniors, unions, walk-ins, or many other classes of customers depending on your business. Keep in mind that the market share of the above segments, along with changes in reimbursement prices, changes constantly, which impacts the dollar size of any market even if the unit volume does not change.

Market Segment by Insurance Carrier (Payer)

Insurance carrier could mean the federal, state, or local government, Medicare/Medicaid, private payer, Medicare supplemental insurance, cash (no insurance), and so on. As you know, prices may vary substantially from one carrier to another, which may impact both sales dollars and units.

Market Segments by Sales and Distribution Channel

Sales and distribution channels could mean established industry distributors, central warehouses of large chain retail stores, direct Internet sales via a company website, direct delivery from a company warehouse to consumers or physician offices, Groupon-like special sales channels, and finally the growing e-commerce segment, including Amazon.com and others. As you know, prices may vary substantially from one channel to another

Market Segments by Product Category

Product category could mean branded or generic products, bulk or individual shipping requirements, kits or individual components, digital or analog, unit dose, or multi-dose, and immediate or controlled release. As you know, prices may vary substantially from one product category to another.

Market Segments by Technology Platform

Technology platform may reflect the use of older technologies over time within a segment. For example, there may be three technology-platform-based segments in the market with an older category from ten years ago shrinking in volume, another from five years ago slowly growing and stabilizing for now before shrinking, and a third representing the newest technology that is growing market share. As you know, prices may vary substantially from one technology platform to another.

Conclusion

Clearly many of the categories discussed above overlap, but in all cases it is important to recognize that all markets are dynamic and continuously changing. The important point here is that you as the manager/entrepreneur need to know, and you need to show your prospective investors that you know, the important strategic movements in the overall market, what they are, why they are changing, and how those strategic movements impact your idea/technology over time. In short you need to know the short- and long-term direction of your target market better than anyone else.

Key Input to Your Strategic Forecast

Once you have defined and simplified this big market picture to highlight your target market segment, the discussion and analysis then moves to a micro customer-sales forecast level to see how those customers, distribution channels, and payers embrace the market changes over time and at what price and volume. Yes, you are correct that such a market/sales analysis takes time to prepare; however, you will need all this knowledge later when your prospective investors challenge you on your revenue assumptions. If you have an exceptionally good idea and you can clearly articulate why the market will embrace your product, people will listen. It is important that you establish a high level of knowledge and credibility in the strategic development of your target market for your prospective investors and all others. You, not they, must be the expert on your market. They need to recognize that you have very carefully done your research, you can support your hypothesis, and your projections are well sourced, rationally applied, and reasonable.

Take Away Items

- Articulate, celebrate and communicate your compelling idea often
- Think long-term and know your target market better than anyone else

- Recognize the difference between a great commercial idea and a truly disruptive invention
- Do careful personal soul searching and make sure your are ready for this ride

CHAPTER 2

THE START-UP PHASE

*This is a long journey so it is wise to plan for
the long-term big picture in all that you do*

The Importance of Strong Intellectual Property

You operate in a competitive worldwide environment and in a regulated industry that requires a substantial capital investment and long lead times to get to the first dollar of product sales.

Think about this challenging business model from the prospective of an outside investor:

- You will need tens of millions of dollars to execute your business plan, with multiple rounds of investment from a number of parties over time.
- It can take as much as five to ten years to get the product to market.
- The risk is high, and the development project could be terminated at any time with a loss of the entire investment.
- The regulatory labeling of the product, which drives your marketing claims, will be established only at the very end of the process, after all the capital has been invested.
- The level of efficacy can be fully established only after a very expensive phase III clinical program near the end of the multiyear process.

- A government agency will decide whether you can go to market once the entire investment has been made.
- The price of the product will be established at the end of the development process. While you will decide your sales price, the medical reimbursement for your product will be subject to the acceptance of private insurance companies, and government medical insurance programs at the federal and state levels.
- Other competing products and technologies will also be in development around the world during the ten-year development process.

Now, compare all this to establishing a retail store or a service business, which have their own challenges but not such a long list of complexities and risk factors. The difference in your industry, however, is that a successful product can generate billions of dollars in annual sales over many years. This is why such a challenging business model is capable of being funding for the right opportunity. The life sciences business is clearly a high-risk, high-reward business, and it is important to understand and manage risk as you learn to understand the potential rewards.

Patents (filings or issued patents) are a means to an end. While they may be trophies and are worth celebrating, you should note that they can be and often are challenged. In litigation, a patent can be broken up, invalidated, or limited in scope, all of which could adversely impact its value. Often it can be a mistake to drop your guard once a patent issues, as if it cannot be broken later by a strong, well-funded, motivated competitor. In one of my former companies we defended a key patent in court with four plaintiffs. The case went on for two years, with a monthly cost that averaged $500,000 per month. We eventually prevailed, and the other parties had to pay penalties and royalties, but the battle was brutal, stressful, and very costly. Patents have one purpose: to provide a market monopoly for a limited time so that the substantial investment in an opportunity can be justified and paid for over time. Such a temporary market monopoly encourages investment, and without protection the investment risk would often be too high to fund the program.

At one point in my career I has responsibility for coordinating the review and recommendation of new product opportunities for a Big Pharma company. We had an average of five new opportunities coming in to us each week, so our volume of incoming opportunities was strong. We also proactively solicited companies worldwide for research compounds of interest that fit with our strategic goals. While we had a good support team, our resources were not unlimited. Our company's strategic plan required that we focus on a key set of therapeutic priorities that fit our plan, as most successful companies do. Depending on a company's particular business plan, it can be looking for opportunities in anti hypertension, dermatology, mental health, pain management, and so on. We applied two initial tests to each opportunity when it came in:

- Step 1: This step was our process to quickly determine if a new prospective opportunity fit with our strategic plan. If it did, we proceeded to the next evaluation test. If not, we graciously thanked the submitting party and passed. Sometimes we passed it on to one of our sister companies for further review.
- Step 2: This step involved a careful review of market protection. I use "market protection" as a broad umbrella that may include trade secrets, trade agreements, and other things in addition to patents and trademarks—recognizing, however, that strong patents present the best protection while they are valid by territory. Let's spend more time on patents.

As we all know, there are large differences in the quality and quantity of patent programs, so let's review some of the issues to consider:

- Is the patent-estate asset based on a provisional patent filing, a fully complete patent application, or an issued patent?
- Does the geographical coverage consist of the United States only, or does the entire patent estate cover all of North America, Europe, and Asia?
- Is the invention broad, so broad that it is at risk of being challenged, or is it just right?

- Is it a composition-of-matter patent or a "picture," or a process patent that a competitor skilled in the art could circumvent?
- Does the patent estate have the benefit of new post filing developments and enhanced discoveries that have been found and filed within the appropriate period to be considered part of the original invention, or is it a filing with no post filing research to discover those special added benefits that enhance the value of the original invention?
- Is the file in the patent office thick with potential prior art and other related inventions, or is it a thin patent file with no other apparent inventions in this area?
- How much practical market-exclusivity life remains with the patents as compared to the development time to get to market? What is the projected net market protection post launch? Is it three, five, seven, or ten years or more?

Note: The following must always be considered.

- Is this patent defensible in its current form? Remember only the most successful inventions get challenged by the competition and can be potentially broken or limited by litigation long after the patent has been issued.
- Does it have an adequate number of true market-protection years to justify the investment required to bring this opportunity to market before generic competition takes it away? Depending on the time left, the development challenges, and the time it will take to get FDA approval, there should be enough market exclusivity to easily justify the investment.
- Does this technology/product have the geographical breadth of protection and global market demand to enable it to be a core strategic investment for a large global player? Remember Big Pharma prefers "global" products to feed its global development and distribution system. It also has a compelling need to replace large, older products that are in decline.
- *Decision:* If the answers to *all* of the above are yes, the evaluation goes to the next step, and I will cover this in more detail later. If

only one or two answers are yes, the evaluation may run the risk of termination at this first screening level, depending on the specific business opportunity. Our policy was to quickly turn down any opportunities that did not pass the initial screen out of courtesy to those companies. As you may already know, not all companies do this, and your package can sit within a company for weeks or months before you receive an answer back from the company.

Forming a Legal Entity for Your Start-Up Company

Company Form
Most start-ups in this industry are C corporations. They may start as S corporations, but once professional investors get involved, they will become C corporations in most situations. There are also situations where it is advisable to have a limited partnership, but without a clear purpose for the limited partnership, most companies will go with the C corporation entity form. An S corporation, if formed by individuals, offers the opportunity to allocate losses directly to the shareholders. This can be a very nice benefit in the beginning, when there are usually losses. Once LLC's or corporations come in as other investors, it is no longer possible to continue the S corporation, which is usually converted to a C corporation. The C Corporation is the most common type of corporation used in this industry. Save yourself the trouble, and find a good corporate/ securities attorney to help you form your legal entity. You will need to use this attorney going forward, so do some research to retain quality legal counsel.

Authorized Capital (Shares)
Typically companies are formed with a number of authorized shares. These may include both preferred stock and common stock classes of equity. They may also involve multiple classes of common and multiple classes of preferred stock. Most companies have one class of common and may or may not authorize preferred stock. It is not

uncommon for a professional investment firm to purchase preferred shares, often when the investor provides a substantial level of financing. If preferred shares are not already authorized, such a change will require approval by the common shareholders. It is often useful at this time to establish a stock option plan allocating a certain number of authorized stock options to be granted with all the appropriate conditions that fairly support management to encourage loyalty and longevity of service, while providing the recipients a strong work incentive to succeed. Keep in mind that all these authorizations can be changed over time with shareholder approval, so make sure you begin with an adequate number of authorized shares so as not to box yourself in later.

Choose a state to incorporate in. Most companies choose their state of residence, and Delaware is often the alternative, given its advanced level of corporate laws, governance issues, and cost. I would avoid incorporating in states with very odd security laws that will only compound and slow down financing discussions later. Keep it simple, especially when you know you will be raising capital from smart, well-informed investors. If your capitalization structure is too complicated, they can use this as an excuse to move to other opportunities and pass up yours. When filing with the state, you establish the authorized number of shares, which is different from the number of shares issued to shareholders. The number of authorized shares becomes more important as more capital is raised, more stock options are granted, and mergers and acquisitions take place. For example, you may file to authorize 100 million common shares. It is possible that you will issue 10-30 million shares to various investors over time. You may also want to reserve 1.5 million underlying shares for use in your new stock option plan. Very often a more definitive stock option plan is negotiated at the time the first professional become investors in the company. It is not unusual for an incentive package to be 15% of the anticipated shares outstanding. It is always useful to start with a larger amount of authorized shares because if you find it necessary to exceed that number in the future, you will be required to first obtain shareholder approval.

Articulating Your Long-Term Business Strategy

There are three common reasons why businesses fail. The first is poor or inexperienced management, the second insufficient funding, and the third focusing on the wrong business strategy. We could say that good management reduces the other two risk factors, and this is why good management is of paramount importance from the very beginning. Smart, experienced investors know this and look for this early in their evaluations.

It is very common for underfunded companies to begin operations but then stall when they are unable to raise capital to continue development and must stop operations. A company stall is one of he worst situations and can be fatal. At a minimum, a stall will substantially reduce pre-money value on the next round of financing.

You might be surprised at the number of companies that fail to get their strategies right, or find themselves changing it annually. First of all, "strategy" refers to long-term goals and understanding the target market for five or ten years or more. "Tactics" refers to the short-term annual objectives and should be considered not strategy but merely the next year's installment of the current strategic plan. The short-term annual operating objectives are designed to meet and integrate with the long-term goals and business strategy.

A strategy statement needs to be simple, easy to understand, and able to be effectively communicated to a wide variety of audiences. It should be thoughtful and supported by strong research driven by market need. Finally, the strategy should be achievable.

Most small start-up companies should have a more focused long-term goal until success and capital formation suggest something broader. It would be silly for a small start-up to declare an objective of being one of the top ten worldwide pharmaceutical companies within ten years. Be energetic and confident, but try to avoid being perceived as ungrounded or, worst case, delusional by your audience. State your long-term strategy clearly, and show your audience you can achieve it as stated, and they will respect you for your honesty, common sense, and mission focus.

Business Model Selection:

You might be surprised how many companies fail to properly articulate their planned business models. The business model simply describes to investors how you plan to make money. Too often it is buried in the presentation while the audience is attempting to figure out what the model really is. Take the time to clearly articulate your business model. Here are some examples:

- Development company: A delivery system technology platform with the intention of licensing/partnering each use of the technology to an existing, well-funded partner.
- Fully integrated company: A fully integrated company that does R&D (research and development) and markets its own products in the United States and possibly outside the United States with or without commercial partners.
- Hybrid: A development company with both technology platforms that can be individually partnered and some individual product opportunities that it intends to develop to later stages. The latter could be partnered in later stages for a greater financial benefit or, alternatively, taken directly to the marketplace.

So why is this important? The answer is simple: depending on your choice, the capital requirements, the management team breadth, and the risk factors all move in different directions.

Example 1: If your plan is to put all your efforts into a promising technology platform with many potential uses, then that choice will send a message that you have a focused business plan with good internal operating leverage. The management team required for this business model is primarily scientific, developmental, and licensing oriented, and the capital required to achieve the first level of success will be lower than if the company took the development project through a full development program through FDA approval and market launch. It also means to the investor that your first partnering deal may occur much sooner than your first dollar of product sales post approval. The other message it sends is that you are focused on a set of key, well-defined licensing objectives, so you have the start-to-finish concept in your business planning.

Example 2: If your plan is to be a fully integrated company, then the investment will be higher, the management team breadth is far more important, the payback may be longer, and the risk is higher simply because the company is taking on execution and funding risk at all levels. On the other hand, the overall long-term payback for an exceptional billion-dollar product opportunity could be enormous.

It is always important to define what/who you are in discussions with other parties to keep the conversation productive and exciting.

Product Pipeline

Your development pipeline should clearly coincide with your long-term business strategy. Highlight the main events because that is where all the investment capital will be applied. Show the early-stage opportunities with an indication of the level of focus they will receive overall so that it is clear you are not wavering from your long-term strategy. If you have five programs in your pipeline, they do not each get 20 percent of all resources, so you need to clarify the optimal level of resources planned by program.

Be realistic about your choices

Be realistic and specific when describing your business strategy. If you have very strong financial backers and a world-class management team with world-class technology, you might have a strategy of being a stand-alone fully integrated company. If so, you will need to continue to raise additional capital over time and have the technology and human resources to directly develop and sell your own products going forward. You might be best described as a development company.

Now if you are not already a class 1 development company, then you will struggle for funding and quality management and will not have the virtual certainty of raising large amounts of capital as needed. You may have some great ideas and inventions, but they may not be considered truly disruptive on a global basis. You will have to partner most, if not all, of your technology, and this reality should be recognized and communicated up front at all times to set the expectations of your audience. With that, you will be evaluated based on your ability to develop and partner rather than take on the major Big Pharma players in the sales and marketing arena—a whole different evaluation. Also, keep in mind that choosing to partner your technology with a larger company does not mean that it is going to offer to acquire you. Your exit may be the result of other programs in your pipeline that lead to another opportunity. Most small emerging companies fall into this development-company category, and all tend to be highly dependent on the success of this first partnering deal.

If you are partnering your technology, it is useful to show more than one opportunity to leverage the desired investment. Your ability to raise capital will rise substantially once a quality partnering deal with a high-profile partner is in place. In a prior life, I joined a company with a $17.5 million market cap, and after we consummated a corporate partnership fourteen months later, the market cap rose to $350 million (a twentyfold increase). Raising capital at that time was clearly not as difficult as it was earlier, and it became easier the more capital we raised. Such conditions make it easier to accelerate promising programs in the pipeline that are capital and human resources constrained. The investment community, which might have ignored these programs prior to the partnership, will now begin to pay attention to them and allocate some/more value to them while lowering the risk of their being partnered in the future. With the right partner and with the right deal in place to benefit your shareholders, you can become a player instead of a beggar overnight. As usual, success begets success.

Here are some examples of typical business-strategy statements (often called mission statements):

- To develop and introduce, directly or through a corporate partner, the most effective therapeutic cancer vaccine to be commercialized in North America, Europe, and key Asian countries
- To develop the first controlled-release oral formulation for [XYZ product category] in the United States, Europe, and Canada, that provides consistent efficacy with a reduced twenty-four-hour side effect profile, and to do so in five years
- To develop and commercialize a disruptive therapeutic service to [XYZ patients] that eventually utilizes a new distribution channel that will capture at least a 20 percent share of patient and physician acceptance by the fourth year of market introduction

Take Away Items

- The worth of your company begins with your patent estate. Strengthen it, protect it, and be prepared to defend it in the future.
- Carefully define your intended business strategy and consistently communicate it,
- Your business model defines how you intend to make money for your investors. Therefore, it must be crystal clear to all internal and 3rd parties.

CHAPTER 3

INITIAL FORMATION OF THE BUSINESS

Build and develop you extended team of executives,
employees, board members and advisors in a manner
that helps you with the difficult challenges ahead

Company Form Determination

In chapter 2 we covered the formation of the legal entity of your new business. By now you should have the legal entity in place with authorized class of equities, authorized shares, and issued shares at a minimum. Hopefully, you have also made the important decision to retain a quality corporate attorney to help you with all securities matters and general business procedures and processes. A good corporate attorney will be able to help you with all business contracts, employment agreements, employee stock option and other incentive programs, fund raising disclosure documents, other contracts involving licensing, acquisitions, mergers, shareholder issues, board of director issues, and general business counsel. Make sure the attorney you choose has the right experience in securities work and general business to help you raise capital and build your business. A good attorney is rarely cheap but will keep you from making common early mistakes and provide you the guidance you should have going forward on general corporate matters that come up often and routinely.

Board of Directors Formation

Every corporation must have a board of directors. The board is elected directly by shareholders, typically on an annual basis, and its primary purpose is to represent the interests of the shareholders. It is typical to authorize an odd number of director positions on the board when forming the legal entity. An odd number prevents tie votes The board is responsible for both recruiting and removing management, when such decisions become necessary to best serve the shareholders.

The board of directors is not an extension of the management team but instead is a higher authority that operates between the shareholders and the management teams, to best serve the interests of all shareholders. All the power and authority granted to management in operating the company comes directly from the board of directors and is subject to change by the board at will. Typically the board appoints a CEO, who in turn forms his/her management team and appoints additional officers of the company, with the prior approval of the board. Additional officers such as vice presidents and the chief financial officer have the authority to bind the legal entity in financial matters. The board also decides on the levels of spending authority it wishes to grant to the CEO and other officers.

In small start-up companies, this relationship is often blurred and overlapping, but it is important to realize its true purpose. All boards evolve over time as the company develops and the shareholder base widens with new capital-formation activities. Often in small start-up companies, the board consists primarily of major shareholders and/or corporate officers/management. As the legal entity grows and formalizes over time, third-party directors will, and should, begin to integrate and change the make up of the board.

The duties of a healthy, productive board are numerous and include some of the following:

- Approving the appointment of all corporate officers, such as the CEO, president, chief financial officer, and corporate secretary

- Filling any board vacancies that might open in between annual shareholder meetings
- Deciding on all corporate development matters, including mergers, acquisitions, divestitures, and technology in-out licensing/partnering
- Hiring/terminating the chief executive officer
- Approving the compensation of the CEO and other key executives, including salary, bonus and equity incentives, and employment contract
- Approving the CEO's compensation recommendations regarding salary changes, bonuses, and equity incentives for all employees
- Reviewing and deciding upon the following:
  - Management's strategic plan recommendation
  - Management's annual goals and objectives
  - Management's annual budget recommendations, including all new employees, capital equipment, spending levels, and timing
  - Spending authority limits for the CEO and management team relative to capital expenditures and operating expenses, leases, and so on
- Determining the need and deciding on the formation of board committees, their purposes, and their makeups

Board Recruitment

Recruit from the best list of business executives you can find that are willing to sit on a board of directors of a start-up company. This configuration works best if you plan to form a scientific/medical advisory committee of the board to advise on scientific/medical matters. You may not initially know all members personally, but what is important is that they have the right business experience and can be strategically supportive to you in achieving your long-term plan. You have to compensate these accomplished executives, and that compensation most often comes in the form of a combination of stock options and cash. Cash is difficult to find in the beginning, so you will have to rely on an attractive stock option package to recruit and retain strong board members.

The right set of quality board members will be able to provide some of the following benefits to the company over the years:

- Advise/caution you against making bad decisions
- Support your best decisions
- Provide a periodic sounding board for ideas and to discuss pending or current problems and opportunities
- Possibly find additional high-quality board members for consideration

In addition, board members may have certain industry contacts involving capital, regulatory, operations, and marketing channels, they may know of some quality future hires that you might consider, and so on.

Experienced board members know that you, the CEO, run the company, and they want to be helpful but not intrusive. In a healthy situation, the board, the CEO, and the management team all want the same thing for the benefit of the shareholders.

Your board directors are counselors first but do not necessarily need to be investors. They may be investors, they usually are, it is best if they are, and if professional investors are involved, they may be major investors in your company. It is always best if board members have some equity to have some skin in the game, so to speak. Should you as an executive ever control the board? Never. As someone said, absolute power corrupts absolutely, which is why the separation is needed. It is also best if the chairman of the board is not the CEO but instead an independent director that is not part of the management team. This separation is not only healthy but is preferred by most securities agencies and exchanges. However, the relationship of the CEO with his/her board is extremely important and has to be one of first trust, then business achievements.

This should never be a "good old' boy" relationship but instead one that is objective and that best serves all the shareholders at all times.

In a healthy board-CEO relationship, your board members should be your best counselors. They represent your shareholders, and they want you to succeed. Their job is not to run your company but to make sure you are running it properly for the benefit of the shareholders. I have always found my boards to be useful, supportive, and sympathetic. With that said, I often would bounce ideas off them, take the time to discuss issues in between board meetings, inform them of bad news quickly, and not surprise them. In short, I tried to treat my board of directors, as I would have wanted to be treated if I were in their position. In return, over time, I earned their trust, and while I did not have control of the board, I was able to control my recommendations and agenda because the board members knew I was truthful and trustworthy, had the best interests of the shareholders in mind, and was dead serious about achieving my business objectives. Here are some thoughts on how to develop a board of directors:

Developing Your Board of Directors
A developing board, which is often an early start-up board, may look like this:

- The chairman is the CEO and possibly the Founder
- Other key operating employee-executives of the Company that currently report directly to the CEO are often represented on the board.
- There are no independent directors on the board.
- Not one board member is an accomplished business executive in a related business.

Such a board configuration is not unusual in a small scientific start-up, but going forward it is problematic and will become burdensome as the company develops and grows. Often some key strategic mistakes are made at this early level simply because the overall breadth of knowledge and experience is missing at the board level. As you raise capital from investors, you become a business, not just a science project. Going forward, it is important to excel technically and financially in order to provide an appropriate return to your shareholders.

At some point an event will force a change at the board level, usually a major funding event involving professional investors. With that event the following might occur:

- The chairman is now the choice of the new lead investor.
- The CEO remains and should always remain on the board as a director.
- The other company executives on the board most likely are asked to resign from the board.
- New board members are added. They might include other investors with large equity stakes.
- Independent business executives with relevant experience are asked to sit on the board.
- The new board requires that the CEO form a scientific/medical advisory team.
- The new board begins to conduct itself in a more disciplined manner given the new capital at risk.
- The new board sets up a number of board committees to serve specific purposes.
- The new board focuses on strategic goals, expense planning, and management objectives.

The Appointment of Corporate Officers

The authority to appoint corporate officers comes directly from the board of directors. Corporate officers have the legal authority to bind the corporation, subject to limits imposed by the board. Each year the board may reappoint officers with titles of chief executive officer, president, corporate secretary, treasurer or chief financial officer. This list just presented represents the common titles but the board could appoint other corporate offices as they see fit. The appointment of offices usually occurs at the first board meeting following the election of new board members by the shareholders.

The authority of officers, as previously mentioned, comes from the board and may be changed periodically at will by the board. For example, the board may authorize spending limits for the CEO that might include something like $200,000 for the total cumulative payments involving any one expense item, $75,000 for capital expenditures, discretionary bonuses of up to $2,500 per employee, etc. As part of a normal financial control system the board may approve similar, but lower level, approvals for some of the other corporate offices. Authorized spending limits are important because the limits make it clear that anything above those limits require full board approval.

Board Committee Formation and Purpose

General

Most boards of directors, especially those that serve or will serve publicly traded companies, form a number of board-authorized committees. Some of those committees are permanent, while others may have a short-term singular purpose. Committees serve a purpose in that they allow a small group with the relevant professional skill set / experience to focus and perform a more thorough analysis on a limited subject. In this way the committee can strive to make a clear, concise evaluation of the subject matter, resulting in a thoughtful recommendation to the full board of directors. Once formed, each committee appoints its own chairman, and the committee serves at the pleasure of the full board of directors, which may make changes to the committee from time to time as the need arises.

Remuneration

It is typical for companies to provide extra compensation to board members that also serve on board committees to fairly compensate them for the additional professional services involved in committee work outside regular board meetings. Often the work done in committee is time consuming and involves areas of specific expertise. Committees do not decide but instead make recommendations back to the full board. The full board decides whether to accept committee recommendations.

Audit Committee

Purpose
The purpose of an audit committee is to ensure that the financial control system that the company operates under is appropriate and acceptable for this company and industry. In a publicly traded company, an audit committee is required, especially by the listing agencies, such as NASDAQ. Typically the full board forms an audit committee and has it chaired by a qualified current member of the full board. That person may or may not be a current board member, but he/she usually is. The important issue is to recruit members that have the specific qualifications to serve on this important committee, even if you need to go outside for such talent. The qualifications for an audit committee member may include years of experience in either public or private accounting as an auditor, controller or higher, CFO (chief financial officer), and so on, or prior experience on the audit committees of other companies, or time employed by federal or state agencies involved in matters of financial integrity. Formal meeting notes/minutes are prepared by the corporate secretary and approved by the committee for future reference.

Responsibilities
The audit committee is responsible for making sure financial controls are established and implemented within the company. Financially qualified specialists normally populate the audit committee. Financial skills are required to interpret financial reports and monitor financial controls. In some companies the audit committee may periodically perform an internal audit in between external audits to make sure management

is properly following the established systems of financial controls. The audit committee recommends the recruitment or continuance of the external auditor and has direct contact with the external auditors at any time. The audit committee is intimately involved in reviewing the external audit report completed during and after the annual audit of the books and participates in all discussions regarding the audit with the external auditors and management, typically the CEO and CFO. The audit committee, like all other committees, reports to the full board of directors with findings and recommendations regarding matters of internal control. The full board, which may include some of the audit committee members, rules on all recommendations made by the audit committee.

The audit committee may also be charged by the full board to establish/review current company policies on reimbursed expenses. Such programs may include travel allowances such as the class of airfare, hotel selections, meal allowances, ground travel transportation guidelines, and entertainment. It is normal for the audit committee to review all expense reports of the CEO and often other highly paid executives for fairness and to ensure that those key executives adhere to company expense-reimbursement guidelines. The audit committee may also be involved in establishing policy recommendations for relocation expenses, educational (tuition) reimbursement, and other policies that apply to all employees.

Compensation Committee

Purpose

In a publicly traded company, a compensation committee is required, especially by the listing agencies. Typically the full board forms an audit committee and has it chaired by a qualified current member of the full board. Qualifications may include years of experience in either public or private accounting as an auditor, controller or higher, CFO, and so on. Membership may also include some outside financial professions qualified to serve on this committee.

Responsibilities

Compensation within a company often involves cash (salary) compensation, periodic bonuses, and profit sharing or equity incentives. Equity incentives could be in the form of special stock grants, the granting of stock options or warrants, 401(k) or other retirement plans, deferred compensation programs, or special purchase-price programs for employers that wish to purchase company stock.

It is especially important that publicly traded companies have formalized compensation programs in all areas. These programs should be documented and in some cases require shareholder approval. The compensation of the CEO and the top group of the highest-paid executives is also a special compensation group that requires special attention.

A typical compensation program recommended by the compensation committee and approved by the full board of directors might include the following:

- Salary changes: Salaries and merit increases are reviewed periodically at a certain time each year, or as needed. This might begin with an overall companywide percentage increase guideline determined by the board. Such a guideline is provided to the CEO, who then makes his/her salary increase recommendations for all employees. It is normal for the board to define a minimum an annual salary that requires Board review, by individual, with all lower annual salaries grouped and summarized with a percentage increase in the aggregate. Obviously, such a procedure varies by the number of employees in the company and changes from time to time. However, in most cases the recommendation from the CEO is, with few exceptions, approved by the board.
- Promotions: The committee/board may choose to provide an overall guideline on salary changes for promotions; otherwise promotions are granted at the discretion of the CEO.
- Appointment of corporate officers: This decision is the responsibility of the full board.

- Salary and cash/stock bonuses: The committee should provide guidelines on matters involving bonus programs. Obviously, a fair amount of discretion is normally afforded to the recommendations of the CEO and the senior management staff. Usually, the committee/board reviews all executive bonuses above a certain level.
- Stock options: Because such programs involve the issuance of securities, it is normal for the committee to set guidelines and for the CEO to make recommendations by employee for such special incentive compensation. Once again the compensation committee normally considers the recommendations of the CEO. The committee normally reviews stock option and warrant contract grants with final approval by the full board based on the committee's recommendations.
- Employee benefit programs: These may include group medical insurance, life insurance, and disability insurance.
- 401(k)/retirement programs: The committee is involved in reviewing the creation of the plan, along with the CEO. The committee recommends certain guidelines to the full board for use in administering the policy to the entire employee population.

Scientific/Medical Advisory Committee

Purpose

There may or may not be an existing scientific/medical advisory committee, but it is often the case that such a committee serves an important strategic purpose in the life science industry. This committee may include key executives, former associates, and so on. The committee's purpose is to validate the strategic worthiness of management's strategic development plan to include its risks and rewards in an effort to keep the board of directors informed as to the quality of the science and technology in development. It is also important to rotate advisors as needed to reflect a committee as it applies to the then-current development pipeline, which may change from year to year. For example, if your pipeline is at the research or preclinical stage, it may include a number of research scientists. Later, as your pipeline matures, you may wish to add development and clinical expertise.

Responsibilities

The committee must have a process to get all the facts so it can provide the very best advice to the company. The CEO is charged with making sure this happens and his/her executives provide full cooperation and full disclosure to the committee at all times.

The role of this committee is to first provide an opinion on the development programs and their objectives. It points out where the independent committee supports and programs and where some disagreement might exist. It identifies risks and communicates its thoughts and findings periodically. The fine details of all this depend on your company and its specific developmental challenges. If the company's focus is on early science, then research advisors are appropriate; if there is a later-stage clinical/regulatory focus, then clinical and regulatory advisors should be involved.

Like any quality support service, committee advisors need to be recruited and compensated, and stock options can provide that compensation to attract the best talent to your committee. Either one of the key advisors can best serve as committee chair. It is probably best for the chair not to be a current executive involved in the development programs. Having said that, it is imperative that the company's developmental executives be deeply involved in providing the committee with detailed information on all developmental programs routinely and fully to be able to obtain, in return, the committee's best thinking on such matters.

Furthermore, it is very important that the executives in charge of development participate in advisory meetings, but it is also important that the committee members have the opportunity to meet periodically in executive session—that is to say, with only committee members—if they wish to do so. This helps to prevent missteps or missed opportunities and allows the committee members to speak freely among themselves on matters that might be awkward in a mixed group. This is only for the common good of the company, and company executives need to understand this principle without being threatened by it.

The committee's comments and recommendations are to be provided periodically to the full board of directors.

Other Special Committees
From time to time various other events and needs arise that may warrant the formation of a special committee to get involved in a more intensive effort to achieve a task required by the full board. Some of these committees might include the following:

- New CEO recruitment committee
  - To determine the qualifications of the next CEO and perform due diligence on the following matters:
  - Seek out qualified executive-recruiting firms, evaluate, decide
  - If internal, interview current team members, evaluate, decide
  - Determine through internal and external means the appropriate compensation package for the new CEO
- New board-director recruitment committee
  - To determine the qualifications of the next board director and perform due diligence on the following matters:
  - Seek out qualified executive-recruiting firms, evaluate, decide
  - If internal, interview current team members, evaluate, decide
  - Determine through internal and external means the appropriate compensation package for the new director
- Fundraising support committee
  - To focus attention on a deal in progress that may take months to conclude
  - To define needs and expectations

- To offer support to management and keep the full board involved when the CEO is time challenged
- Merger/acquisition/partnering (major transaction) committee
  - To focus attention on a deal in progress that may take months to conclude with many complexities
  - To offer support to management and keep the full board involved when the CEO is time challenged

Take Away Items

- Effective Corporate governance is always important. The relationship you have with your shareholders and the Board is something that you always want to strengthen and maintain for a healthy working relationship.
- Be thoughtful in forming your Board with the long-term needs of the company in mind at all times.
- Board committees can be very useful in managing relations with your Board. Remember that the committee work and final recommendations will always come to the full board for a final decision and establishing good consensus at the committee level is the first step. Keep in mind that publicly traded companies will require certain committee such as audit and compensation.
- Use special, temporary committees when the need arises as this can be very helpful in calming the nerves of board members during the process of completing a major transaction and some other major event.

CHAPTER 4

FUNDING / CAPITAL FORMATION

Fundraising is an ongoing process, not an event.

I t is easy to devote an entire book to the various fundraising challenges and opportunities. Fundraising, like most things we do, is both a science and an art—*you need to be good at both to be successful.* In this chapter I attempt to cover many of the basics to help you better prepare and present yourself and your company to the appropriate funding sources.

Fundraising has much to do with the potential of your technology and the reputation of the CEO and board. If your technology is recognized as clearly disruptive, you are in great shape. If the company CEO comes with a track record of previous successes and has made a number of venture or institutional investors money in the past, then the company is also in great shape. If you have a star CEO and a star disruptive technology, you can fast forward through most of what I am going to describe below, and go to major institutional sources from day 1 to finance your company's business plan.

The Management Factor in Fundraising

Companies and technologies do not develop by themselves. Keep in mind that investors are buying the company package with a technology, a CEO, and a management team. Here are a few thoughts on management's role in fundraising:

- Investors buy the jockey, not the horse.
- Investors would rather support a Grade A management team with a Grade B technology or product, than a Grade B management team with a Grade A technology/product.
- If you think you or your company's technology platform or product is the only part of your business under investigation, you are mistaken. In reality the investors' perception of your strength as CEO and that of the management team you built is often the primary reason to invest or not. Remember the quality of your management team is a reflection of your leadership skills and your ability to recruit high-quality talent. Also keep in mind that much of the communication between you and your prospective investor in this sensitive area is *deafeningly* nonverbal. You may not know what hit you, and no one will tell you, but this is one of the most common reasons for a turn down or pass on your investment opportunity—and yet it is seldom communicated in words.
- When meeting with investors, consider this advice given to me by a wise, experienced man a long time ago:
  - First, sell yourself (as a capable CEO, a serious person with integrity, a leader—sell your past successes).
  - Second, sell your technology/product.
  - Third, sell your company, in that order

Note: If investors are not impressed with you and what you have achieved to date, the rest of it does not matter. This is especially true in a small start-up company with few resources.

Some Food for Thought to Consider:

- The pain of dilution pales in comparison to the pain of stalling, the result of running out of cash
- Based on your current burn rate, if you have less than 12 months of cash on hand you are already considered shark bait. This rule

does not always apply if your lead investors are high quality, well-respected players.

- The time to raise cash is when you have cash, not when you don't
- Raise cash when the markets are favorable and you are able to raise capital, not when you want to.
- Be mindful of dilution but don't be obsessed with it. More CEO's have ruined their business prospects by running out of cash because they were too obsessed with dilution. This is a rooky mistake, do your best avoid it.
- You will be more successful controlling the business with high quality achievements, than the share count you own.
- 10% of a successful company is always much better than 100% of a failed company.

Preparing Your Company for Fundraising

In our industry, fundraising is a strategic exercise, not a tactical exercise. Fundraising is never performed once and is always an ongoing effort and a challenge. What you do and how you do it in the early rounds, to include the conditions of those financing rounds, will always impact later rounds. It is important to avoid complicating control features and complex capitalization structures. Investors like clean, uncomplicated deals and capital structures that don't require a time-consuming fix. In general experienced investors will simply not invest in complicated deals unless they can restructure them to be simple to facilitate future required funding rounds with new sets of investors.

It is best to retain a professional that understands the process from this start-up phase through an IPO (initial public offering) for best results. As mentioned before, fundraising is a building block approach to a strategic goal; it is not a single task and should never be viewed as a one-off task. You will be raising funds at all times to enable you to fund your strategic business plan.

Private *Placement Memorandum* (PPM)

A PPM is not a selling document but instead it is a legal full-disclosure document that addresses all the key areas of the company, including the bad and the good. A PPM is not a business plan, and it is not a financial projection of your business. The PPM needs to be prepared fully and properly, and it should include a number of risk factors that might apply to this investment. Keep in mind that a PPM is not a selling document but instead a full-disclosure document. Thus, projections should not be part of this document; rather, it should include past financial performance. It is important that you disclose certain risk factors to investors that by their very nature and purpose show investors many reasons why they may not want to invest in your company. You do all this to prevent lawsuits later by investors that feel they were misled by management regarding the investment opportunity.

The initial PPM will take some time to prepare, and it is best to involve experienced professionals to help you develop it and review the final version before releasing it to investors. This is a good time to retain the services of a good corporate/securities attorney for final review. The document needs to be prepared by a person that has done it before, if not an attorney, usually someone with a financial background or prior experience in participating in fundraising efforts. Your PPM will be developed to disclose much of the following:

- Business mission
- Management team and bios
- Development plan
- Key milestones / development phases
- Major commercial agreements / leases in place
- Employment contracts, or lack thereof
- Capitalization structure
- Patents and other intellectual property
- Current or pending litigation
- Financial statements (from inception)
- Use of proceeds of this financing (with offering expenses)

As you prepare the PPM draft, it is useful to begin developing an electronic data library that includes the actual full contracts, with all attachments, for all the material agreements mentioned in the PPM. Both the PPM and the data library may be required to satisfy the due diligence of prospective investors or investor groups and/or their representatives.

It is important to note that most PPM's are what are called "Reg. D offerings," which refers to a certain section of federal securities act that covers such private investments to individuals. Again, you should work with an experienced securities attorney on this effort. PPMs should be sent not to general public investors but instead to more sophisticate investors that you know that are accredited investors who meet certain financial guidelines as determined by law and the Securities and Exchange Commission (SEC).

Company-Overview Presentation

You will need to develop a separate company-overview presentation to sell your business plan. The PPM is not a selling document but a matter-of-fact disclosure document, and you should avoid making any projections (financial or otherwise) in your PPM. Your company overview is usually a slide deck, thoughtfully prepared, short, and hard hitting. Try to keep it to ten to fifteen slides. It should provide all the key investment highlights; avoid being too long and detailed. There will be plenty of time to go over all the fine details during a due diligence process, if the conversation goes that far. This document is often e-mailed to prospects, giving them a quick sense of what the company is all about so that they can determine whether they wish to proceed any further with their analyses. It is always best to get experienced, professional help in developing, or at least reviewing, final versions of these important documents. In other situations, it can be useful to prepare a one-page highlights brochure that summarizes the compelling reasons to invest in your company. This brochure can also be used to e-mail company information to prospects that wish to learn a little bit more about the investment opportunity to see whether the investment is a fit for their firms.

Potential Sources of Funding

There are many sources of funding available for the average start-up company. The following sections describe several of them.

Founder's Stage

You have your great idea and you have completed a great deal of work in supporting your business thesis as to why this great idea will be successful. Let's get started.

First, you need to form your corporation and you can do this be either retaining a corporate securities attorney, or going to an online firm such as legalzoom.com to have them assist you in doing the formation, or going to the state website for corporations and doing the formation on line. Fees are generally $200-300 and any legal services can be $200-600 depending on the complexity of your corporation. You will need to get a federal EIN number in the process. During this process you will initially appoint yourself as the President, CEO, Corporate Secretary and Treasurer and board director, until you have others to handle those roles. Let's assume you authorize the corporation for 20,000,000 common shares.

Second, write a check to the newly formed corporation for the shares you intend to issue to yourself. Let's assume you write a check for $1,000 and you buy yourself 1,000,000 shares at the par value of $.001 per share. You will need your federal EIN number to open the corporate bank account.

Congratulations founder! You now have a corporation with authorized shares, a board of director(s), corporate officers appointed, a bank account and a small amount of cash in the bank. You also use this cash to reimburse yourself for any costs of forming the company and leave the balance. Now if you have not completed your PPM and corporate overview and any other supportive material, it is now time to do so to prepare for your discussions with you prospective seed investors to discuss your great idea.

Seed Stage

This is often a more informal stage and your seed investors tend to be family, friends and close associates that know you well. Funding at this stage group often occurs based on trust, confidence in you personally, and a well thought out story. Keep in mind that your seed investors are the ones that are taking the highest risk at such an early stage. You will present your business case and provide the PPM and support for your business plan/thesis to these investors in private meetings. Let's presume that you have a need to raise $200,000 in seed capital and you are successful in selling 200,000 new shares for $1.00 per share to the seed investor group. So when the seed round is closed you should have $200,000 in cash in the bank and 1,200,000 common shares outstanding. With this capital raise you defined how you are going to use the $200,000 and that most likely includes filing patents, additional patent(s) prosecution in the US and in key territories of the world. You may also have plans to conduct certain pre-clinical trials in animal models, or market research, or other important matters to further support your business hypothesis for the next round of financing. If you planned to take a small salary during this phase you will need to disclose that in the Use of Proceeds section in your PPM along with any payroll tax expense that the company will need to pay.

Special Funding Programs

- Government/private grant programs
- Small business loans (with your guarantee)

This group is not informal, but it is less formal than other sources. All government grant programs have strict procedures for applying for grants. They require a prepared plan with appropriate justification. In the case of a small business loan, a bank will most likely require you to personally guarantee the loan at this early stage. These programs take time, they are competitive, and you cannot count on such grants alone to build your business. Use this source only if it fits with your plans and enables you to establish an important milestone or two for future use.

Angel Financing

- Individual angel investors: high-net-worth individuals that are willing to invest in emerging companies
- Angel network forums: organized groups of angel investors that meet periodically and during such meetings invite four to six CEOs to present to the group as a whole.

You are now beginning to sell your business plan to independent third-party investors. During this phase you will be required to prepare a quality company-overview presentation to present (sell) your story to investors. In addition, you will be required to prepare a formal private placement memorandum (PPM), which is a full-disclosure document for prospective investors. Typically, the company overview first allows the investor to determine whether this investment fits his/her investment profile. If there is interest, you send the investor a PPM, and after a number of discussions, if there is further interest, a formal due diligence process on the part of the investor begins.

Before you begin this process, you should first be honest about the level of funding you need to get through the next phase/milestone that you expect investors to support. Most companies fail or stall, which often leads to failure, because they did not properly plan for their true funding needs and fell short too soon in the process. This is all about planning, and it is usually a management failure, so be mindful of this as such an event will become part of your history that has to be explained to some other prospective investor in the future.

If you need $50K to $150K to reach your next major development milestone, you might be able to accomplish this with the help of a couple of motivated angel investors. Given the need for large amounts of capital in your industry if you really need at least $1 million to $2 million, to achieve that next important milestone. If so you should do it right the first time and consider skipping the interim angel step and soliciting an organized angel investor network in your region of the country and raising the entire amount through that network. Be mindful of the fact that the deal you put in place for the $50K to $150K offering could negatively impact the larger funding effort. An alternative would be to make the very first part of the offering automatically convertible into the larger overall offering. This way you can accomplish a short-term funding need all in one offering.

The investors in that first segment of the financing are justified in receiving a risk premium since the large offering may never happen. Therefore, it is best to avoid the first smaller funding if you really need the larger funding effort, which is most often the case. Keep in mind that you will be raising money in the future, as in normal in our industry. The offerings and the structures of those offerings closed in the past will also impact future offerings. Therefore, it is important to avoid special clauses and accommodations that will be problematic going forward. Anticipate that fundraising will take time and a lot of effort, so if you need cash quickly, you have a problem. The time to begin preparation for the next round of financing is the day after the current round of financing closes. Fundraising never rests.

Venture Financing

General

For the purpose of this discussion, "venture funds" refers to early-stage funding sources that accept higher levels of risk for a potentially higher reward. You will find when working with all classes of funding sources that there is the usual bell curve, where a small group is exceptionally good, a small group is poor and could hurt you in the long run, and everybody else is in the middle. Working with venture funds is no exception, and they are often, fairly or unfairly, referred to as "vulture funds." Venture funds are organizations typically make a very early investment, when the risks are high. These firms also tend to be more patient with the exit phase, knowing that an exit can and will take years to be achieved, and the very best firms are managed and staffed by some exceptionally smart and experienced people.

What you really want is a venture fund that will be your lead investor on behalf of the company and, of course, its own investment. Expect the venture fund to want to understand the full amount of capital needed and to expect you to define operating milestones that correspond with various levels of funding. It is common for a round of funding to correspond with meeting/funding a very specific operating objective. An example of such an objective is to file an IND and conduct a phase I clinical trial. Also, keep in mind that this lead venture fund may take a small round-one investment to establish its equity position at a favorable price. Once that round is closed, its most likely will take the lead in preparing for round two. It is expected to take a small piece of the round-two offering as a show of good will to the round-two investors, and at the higher round-two share price.

This process of successive financing rounds with (hopefully) higher share prices (pre-money valuations) each time is desirable in capital formation. You need to understand this and also that the venture fund you choose is more of a lead capital-formation partner in the long run than it is a primary funding source. You let it into the company on favorable equity-price terms to incentivize it to take your company forward. Though you give up a good percentage of the company in the first round, you will find that if you deliver achievements, the valuation of the company will continue to rise and your lower equity position will be worth much more over time. Your funding risk will also lower dramatically, and that is a very important component of successfully building a life science company to avoid a stall. Too many CEOs decide on a venture investment on the basis of the initial level of funding involved and the pre money valuation it provides to the company. That is often the wrong way to decide on this matter. Finding the very best venture partner who has a solid reputation, can lead future rounds of financing, and will stick with you all the way (assuming you achieve your part) should be your primary decision criterion. Many companies stall and subsequently fail because their funding programs failed.

The fund typically recruits professionals to manage its investment portfolio for the benefit of its investors. These funds often build through investments from pension funds, large institutions, wealthy individuals, or family trusts. Small investors typically do not fund venture funds. The professionals you will meet are hired by the fund to manage it and produce an above-average return for its investors. The return must be above average because the risk investors take is above average. Usually, the fund managers are compensated in part by a portion of the profits generated from the investments they make on behalf of the fund. Often the funds are not the managers' capital, but part of it could be. In any event, the fund managers have a vested interest in making investments that benefit the fund's investor base, and their job is to find the very best investment opportunities and weed out the rest. Most funds have a mission and a focus list of investments that fit a profile approved by their investors. It is important to know a fund's focus to make sure it is a fit for your particular investment. For example, if a fund's mission is to invest in exciting new medical-device technologies and products, it most likely will not be interested in a long-term research program for a new therapeutic category.

Venture funds also tend to specialize in certain areas. Some venture funds may focus on early research opportunities, some pre-IND, and others clinical stage. Often they will focus on certain industries, including therapeutics, diagnostics, devices, biologics, consumer products, health care services, distribution platforms, animal health, and other categories of interest that fit their internal investment profiles approved by their investors.

Top-Tier Venture Funds

If you able to capture the interest of the top-tier venture funds, it will be a long-term blessing to you. If you have that star CEO and that truly disruptive global technology, you most likely are a candidate. What matters is being able to partner with a leading firm with an outstanding record of achievement. A smart, experienced CEO who has done this before knows that it is not the pre money valuation, or the investment amount the venture fund offers you that are the key issue. Instead, it is the quality of the firm, its reputation, its deep pockets for follow-on funding in subsequent rounds, its ability to help you build your team and develop your technology, and finally its ability to help you (and itself) with the final exit, with top underwriters in the case of an IPO.

It is not uncommon for a top-tier venture fund to almost automatically draw interest from other firms. For example, the top-tier venture fund ABC Ventures is investing in biotech company XYZ. ABC Ventures is known for performing outstanding due diligence and has a reputation for having a high-quality understanding of trends in strategic biotech opportunities. Once ABC Ventures is in your company as an investor, its next step is to prepare for the next round of funding. Fund JKL is a big fan of ABC Ventures, having successfully invested in its early-stage deals several times in the past. If the next round of funding is $5 million, then the JKL fund may be quite keen to invest $1 million or $2 million in this next round simply because ABC took the risk and put its "skin in the game." In this case, JKL could be another venture fund or an insurance company or other institutional investor. This, of course, would be subject to JKL completing its own due diligence, but it is probably half way there. So you see from this example how going with quality can make a difference in future rounds of funding. Also, it is important to mention that the normal process in such funding rounds is to increase the pre money valuation each time. It might be $10 per share in the first round, $12 to $15 per share in the second round, and higher thereafter, as an example.

Middle-Tier Venture Funds

Most companies operate within the middle tier, and of course, you want to be at the higher end of the middle tier. Seek a venture investor whose investment profile is a solid fit with your mission. You want a fund that has deep pockets and whose management has sufficient investment experience and leadership to support you during the next several rounds of financing. Remember investor relationships are like marriages except that you cannot fire or divorce an investor. Make good choices for all the right strategic reasons, not just valuation and dilution.

Lower-End Venture Funds

These funds may be new funds that are building their reputations in the industry, or they may have been around with a less impressive track record. They tend to have a lower overall portfolio value and, for a number of reasons, will not have the leadership power to easily command other venture funds to join them in an offering. Another issue you may encounter with lower-tier funds is that they make one investment but may not be able or choose to invest further in later rounds at higher equity prices.

Institutional Financing

These funds tend to be pension funds, corporate money, private equity funds, insurance companies, and so on. These funding sources tend to be governed by much more conservative investment profiles than are found in venture funds. Many of the above issues involving venture firms also apply to institutional funds with regard to reputation, leadership, participation, longevity, and so on. The quest for quality investors should always be a strong priority even at the expense of dilution. In the end the best investor base usually will provide the best exit to all shareholders, including management. Some institutional funds that have worked out some special investment flexibilities may often work with certain venture funds on early-stage investments. I have experienced this with at least one successful venture start-up, and in the end the insurance company made a handsome profit after the IPO. Like all investor groups, institutional funds like to work with other institutional firms that they respect. Some call this teamwork; others may refer to it as a wolf pack. Either way, the concept of investing with a group in a defined round of financing with predefined milestones is fairly routine.

Mezzanine Financing

Institutional investors may also be involved in later mezzanine financing. Mezzanine financing is often a larger amount of financing raised by more conservative investors once you have achieved some key operating milestones. Mezzanine financing often precedes a major funding event, such as an IPO or a pending merger or acquisition. Again, if you secured top venture and institutional investors earlier, this will go much easier and at a much more favorable valuation than if you are working with relatively unknown professional investors.

The IPO and the Role of the Lead Underwriter

Eventually conditions may be right to consider taking your company public. Don't kid yourself, because being a public company can be either a benefit or a curse. For now let's focus on the benefit side.

Underwriters are useful in many ways, but the most common use of an underwriter is to lead financing, be it private or a public offering by way of an IPO. Along the way with venture and institutional funding, we have seen underwriting take place, but it is a much more formal, defined process at this level. For private financing the services of an underwriter can be used for institutional financing and/or mezzanine financing. Underwriters are compensated with a percentage discount of your offering price, expense reimbursement, and finally, stock options and/or warrants. This is normal, so expect it and regard it as one of the many incentives required to make things happen in the financial system.

Again, the quality and reputation of an underwriter is extremely important, and now is when all the work you have done to pick the best venture firms, the best institutional firms, and so on pays off. There is a huge benefit in having a first-tier underwriter such as Goldman Sachs or Morgan Stanley in the form of valuation, lower funding risk, aftermarket support, reputation, pedigree, and so on. Most firms never get this chance, and only the very large firms with the best prospects for success will meet their criteria. On the other hand, if your investor base and your achievements to date allow you to work only with a third-tier underwriter, the story will be quite different in terms of financing risk, valuation, aftermarket support, and so on.

Meet with several underwriters to determine the best fit for both sides, and then negotiate an engagement to conduct the offering.

Depending on the quality of your deal, either you will be selling them or they will be selling you. When you conduct an offering to the public, you have a higher regulatory hurdle because agencies like the SEC are now making sure the average public investor is protected. The SEC is less concerned about professional investors, or accredited investors, as they are often referred to, because these investors have the experience, knowledge, and funds to retain professionals to advise them on such investments. Essentially they are big boys and can and should take care of themselves. However, in a public offering, you are selling shares of your company to all levels of investors with or without sufficient levels of knowledge about your industry, your company, and the terms of your offering, so the SEC plays a role to protect the average public shareholder. Some steps involved are similar to previous steps but with a higher degree of exposure and scrutiny.

Preparing the S-1

Your underwriter will insist on you retaining a high-quality law firm to finalize your S-1, your first regulatory submission. You should consider your PPM to be an early, less detailed version of your S-1, and it is always best to maintain a high level of disclosure in your future PPMs so that there are no surprises along the way. You and your management team will spend a great deal of time drafting and modifying your S-1 with the aid of your attorneys, public accountants, and underwriters. Your S-1 necessarily discloses all the good and bad from your company's past, so always keep this in mind. Every material thing you do from your first day of operation may need to be disclosed, and you may have to explain all of it to prospective investors and underwriters. Your underwriter will insist on audited financial statements for a certain number of years, and your external public accounting firm will participate in the review of this document.

Essentially, management, usually your chief financial officer, prepares the initial draft of the S-1, and then various other parties review and make comments in an effort to get the S-1 to a very high level of full disclosure. After many rounds of comments involving corporate attorneys, public accountants, patent attorneys, underwriters, management, and other professions required depending on the nature of your company and offering, the S-1 will eventually be ready to submit to the SEC.

Once the SEC receives your S-1, its own internal regulatory review begins, and rounds of comments between the SEC and the company continue until the SEC is satisfied, without any deadline on its part to complete the review. When you have addressed all SEC comments to the SEC's satisfaction, the process is completed, and the SEC usually declares the offering effective. SEC effectiveness does not imply approval but instead means the language of your document is sufficiently clear to offer securities to the average public investor for a period of time and subject to no major changes or additional disclosures involving the company. If management has misrepresented the facts in the S-1, then management is responsible for the consequences.

The IPO Road Show

Your underwriter sets up a number of meetings with prospective investor groups to introduce them to the management team and the company plans. This road show follows a parallel process of preparing a company-overview presentation that coincides with the S-1 disclosures. This road show to introduce the company to the investment community often takes three weeks of intensive travel and meeting schedules and is a necessary part of the IPO process. Your underwriter has the objective of funding your IPO with a combination of institutional and public investors. Along the way you also present to retail stockbrokers and institutional fund managers, all of whom will ask plenty of detailed questions about you and your company. This activity is often supported by a draft version of the S-1 printed with disclaimers, often referred to as the "red herring" because the disclaimers are usually printed in red. The disclaimers indicate that the S-1 is under SEC review and is subject to change.

The Underwriting Group: The Syndicate

Your underwriter is the lead underwriter, who controls the book and brings in a number of other financial/underwriting groups, who collectively fund the deal. The book involves a range of shares to be sold at a range of prices, and the lead underwriter allocates shares to the underwriting group of professionals as it sees fit.

The underwriter also works with the various securities exchanges to determine what exchange the company's shares will be listed on. Given that each exchange has its own listing and maintenance rules, the underwriter must make sure the S-1 has been prepared with all this in mind. Most often the exchange will be within the NASDAQ network, with the larger exchanges such as the NYSE reserved for only the very top tier.

Compensating the Underwriter

The lead underwriter typically receives between 5 and 10 percent commission on an equity offering, with smaller deals having a larger commission and larger deals having a smaller commission. In addition, stock options/warrants are usually granted to the underwriter, and the offering often involves a "green shoe" component. The green shoe is often a thirty-day option for the underwriter to sell an additional 10 to 15 percent of the offering at the original IPO price. This creates an incentive for the underwriter and additional capital for the issuer (the company). The lead underwriter determines the compensation allocated to the other members of the underwriting group, which involves the allocation of primary shares in the offering, stock options/warrants, and the contingent green shoe offering.

Pricing/Closing the Deal

At some point the S-1, SEC review, and road show process is complete, and the underwriter is now in a position to recommend to company management what number of shares can be sold with confidence and at what price. This judgment comes after a number of meetings and discussions with all the groups involved in the underwriting process and after level-of-interest discussions with prospective investors. At this point the underwriter may agree to a firm offering or a best efforts offering. In a firm offering, the underwriter agrees to buy all the shares in the offering with the intention of distributing them, or the large majority of them, within the underwriting group. A best efforts offering is just that: a price is set with a share limit, and the market determines the level of funding. Usually underwriting pricing takes place in the evening, along with lots of discussions with investors, with the actual IPO sale of shares taking place just prior to or at market opening. At this stage a specific number of shares are sold at a price agreed upon by the lead underwriter and the company, and distributed to the various brokerage firms involved in the syndicate. The company and the underwriter will have previously arranged for an exchange to trade your newly issued shares with a unique symbol through previously arranged market makers. When all this is completed, your new company shares are now trading publicly.

Note: Most underwriters require a share-selling restriction agreement for a six-month period after the IPO. This usually applies to all insiders (management) and may include some early investors. This restrictive period helps develop a proper market for your company shares.

Post Offering Market Support

So now you have a group of new shareholders that includes small average public shareholders and perhaps some new institutional investors. If your share price dramatically rises to a premium price after trading begins, an investor could choose to take, or flip, a nice profit. The underwriter wishes to be able to sell the green shoe shares and attempts to maintain an orderly market to raise additional capital for the company. This additional capital can only help to bolster the financial strength of the company. The entire syndicate has a vested interest in establishing an orderly market for your shares to enable the green shoe to close within the option period.

Secondary/Follow-On Financing

Often fundraising is an ongoing event. It is possible that your IPO enabled you to completely fund the strategic plan for your company. Or you might need for more capital. If so, consider secondary offerings.

This is when having a quality underwriter again has its benefits. Let's say you need to raise an additional $5 million to $10 million in equity for a special deal or opportunity. You are now a publicly traded company, and hopefully, your company trades well, meaning it has good consistent volume with a steady price level. You might have two choices available:

Secondary Public Offering of Shares

You can conduct another offering to the public, like an IPO, but with less drama since you are already public. You have to prepare another disclosure document for investors and for SEC review. You hold management meetings with your underwriter and prospective investors, and at the end of the new road show, the underwriter makes a pricing recommendation based on investor feedback and completes the offering. These shares, when issued, are free trading with no restrictions for the investors.

PIPE Offering

PIPE stands for "private investment in a public entity." PIPEs are often issued to raise cash faster and a bit more easily by issuing shares to institutions or a group of accredited investors. Often the PIPE involves the issuance of unregistered shares at a discount to the market. The company is responsible for diligently filing a registration statement with the SEC to register these newly issued shares so that the investors can legally sell them in the public market. Shares purchased in a private like a PIPE offering typically are not registered which means those shares cannot be freely sold on the public market until they are registered. Investors take time risk because they have to wait until the company files a registration statement with the SEC for those shares then wait an additional period of time until the SEC declares that registration effective. Once the SEC declares the registration statement for those new shares effective they can be sold on the public market, but not before. For this reason shares are typically sold at a discount to the public market price.

Hypothetical Capital Formation Program

By way of illustration Table A reports a hypothetical capital formation program for the ABC Biotech Company. It begins with a Founders round, shortly thereafter there is a Seed round for $200,000 with family and friends. The next round involves profession investors that place $2,000,000 as professional Round One. This subsequently might be followed by three additional professional rounds at increasing share prices because the ABC Company has done so well in achieving their milestones. After four professional rounds a total of over $30 million was raised and the number of issued and outstanding shares amounted to just under 10.5 million. The table below does not reflect the 1.5 stock options issued to the executive team.

ABC Biotech Company Capital Formation Program			
Funding Round	Capital Raised	Share Price	Shares Issued
Founder Round/Start-Up	1,000	$0.001	1,000,000
Seed Round Investors	200,000	$1.000	200,000
Round One	2,000,000	$1.250	1,600,000
Round Two	4,000,000	$2.000	2,000,000
Round Three	8,000,000	$3.250	2,461,538
Round Four	16,000,000	$5.000	3,200,000
Total	30,201,000	2.887	10,461,538

*For simplicity sake the stock options are not included in the above table. Those stock options were used to attract and incentivize key employees/advisors/consultants to join the company, contribute their exceptional talents and achieve the strategic goals of the company. Stock options are granted over time at varying strike prices (share exercise price) as key people join the company.

We will use this capital formation table later in another chapter.

Take Away Items

- Capital formation, in this industry, is a never ending activity that demands your personal attention and your personal involvement throughout the life of the company
- Invest your time finding the best strategic investors that will help you raise capital in all the later financing stages, for best results.
- Avoid early investors that just provide cash and no strategic capital formation network value even if their deal proposal appears to be better or less dilutive to you near term.
- Use seasoned professionals, part-time if necessary, at all times when raising capital.
- Recognize that your key investors are your partners, probably for life. Work with them as you both have a common strategic interest in this business venture.
- Fund raising takes on different forms and structures as your company develops so work closely with your professionals and advisors for best results.

CHAPTER 5

ORGANIZATIONAL DEVELOPMENT

*Every company has its own culture along
with many moving parts that
need to be maintained continuously.*

Operational Resources

Buildings/Space

At this early stage in your development, the last thing you need is a fancy office or high-priced development center. If you get through the early phase of your business, there will be time for that later, when you have the support of financial advocates. The one thing that will surely turn off the investor in me every time is seeing a CEO spending money for image. I believe most investors would agree with me. What you need is adequate space, good equipment, and good people to do the early work needed to advance your technology to the next step, which is often a funding milestone. If you succeed in obtaining the next level of financing, with it will come the funding necessary to move to a larger lab, development center, and so on. This is not the time to spend valuable cash on frivolous items for image.

Equipment

We are in the technology business, so we require talented people, but we also require sophisticated equipment in addition to standard equipment. If your development work routinely requires sophisticated analytical equipment, then plan for it and get the best equipment you need so that your success is not impaired by the lack of quality resources.

Special Facilities

You may find it necessary to have a special infectious disease containment lab to handle the special needs of your technology, or a vivarium for animal testing, or a special cell line incubation system, or special chemical synthesis equipment that might be needed earlier in the process to manufacture Phase I clinical supplies for human testing. All special facilities need special attention and like everything else need to be properly funded, properly designed and constructed, and managed effectively and safely. Very often special facilities are key to achieving some of the most important business objectives.

Other Capital Items

Depending on your particular business, you may need tools, supplies, some inventory, computers, printers, shelves, files, facility/leasehold improvements, and so on. You must define these in your plan and set the budget for and the timing of such expenditures.

Developing Your Product/Idea

It has been my experience that a management team that always has a plan B remains successful. Unless you are a very lucky person, you should anticipate that certain assumptions made in your business plan would have a different, most likely unfavorable outcome. Call it what you will, but things happens, bad things happen to good people, and so on. The bottom line is that you need to presume things will go wrong and trip you up. It happens to all of us.

Development Risk Management

As the maestro of this development plan, you must be keenly aware of what key components of your plan could change or fail, and you need to worry about these issues. Furthermore, for each possible failure in the plan, you should have a plan B that immediately goes into effect once something fails, and it will. A management team without a plan B is not a first-tier management team. You need to distinguish between assumptions that can go wrong and the unexpected, or black swan events. While you cannot plan for a black swan event, you certainly can plan on the failure of a major assumption in the strategic plan, and you should. So with this message, I want to begin this section by pointing out that your plan will never be perfect, it will never be executed exactly as planned, it will have assumptions that fail, and you will have to fix your plan on the run. Planning for the possibility of failures is a necessary part of good planning. Being blindsided is not expected from a top-tier management team. You monitor risk by periodically revising your plan and questioning the details of all the key assumptions. Your team will take this as seriously as you do.

Success Management: Increasing Your Odds of Success

In life as in all things, you increase your chances of success in an endeavor by doing a good job on growth drivers while also protecting against things inevitably going wrong. In the previous section, I addressed the need to manage risk, and in this section, I will address those management processes that should help to increase your chances of success. Here are some thoughts on this matter:

- Target market: Success management first starts with really understanding your key strategic market opportunities. If you are wrong on this one, you may be developing a product nobody wants or needs.
- Best solution: Next you need to make sure you are developing the best technology or product for that carefully defined strategic market need. You should always worry about this question: Is someone smarter than me developing a better idea?

- Critical success factors: Every business has a set of *critical success factors* that if not executed properly will impair success or cause failure. These factors might involve critical standards for R&D and clinical and regulatory affairs. It may involve standards regarding customer care, product quality, service time, price-value relationships, staff recruiting, employee training, and compensation. Are you focused on everything, or are you focused on all the right priorities? It has been my experience that focus is underrated. Focus often is one of the key reasons for success as it coordinates the entire strength of an organization in a synergistic manner. Creating synergy can be incredibly powerful and effective. Define these critical success factors, write them down, and communicate them often and widely throughout your organization. Make it part of your culture, mean it, and show you mean it through actions, not just words.

- Human resources: Do you currently have the very best management team to accomplish this strategic objective? Do you need to upgrade? Where, who, when?

- Other resources: Will a planning failure on your part to anticipate the proper level of resources, such as equipment, inventory, and third-party support services, occur and trip up your plan?

- Financial resources: Are you being realistic about how much capital you really need, within the time frames indicated in your plan, and at the speed at which you are developing/spending? Are you raising what funds you can, even if there is a capital shortfall, but continuing to spend on the hope the shortfall will be eliminated soon? This can be a very big mistake. It is important to balance your spending with the level of funding you can realistically achieve. You will find that it becomes necessary to slow down or speed up spending during different times in your journey of building your company. Know the difference and make spending adjustments as needed to protect your cash at all times. Avoid a company stall involving the life-threatening exhaustion of cash at all times. Cash is still king, and it always will be!

- Control/dilution: Are you too concerned with losing control or incurring dilution at the expense of sacrificing the quality or timing of your key business goals, some of which are market driven with timing sensitivities?

- Commitment to planning: Is proper business planning just a feel-good exercise, or is it the tool you, as the CEO, really count on to drive the growth of your company? How often do you update your plan? Annually? Quarterly? How often do key components of your plan change? Are the strategic goals in your strategic plan, and the specific management objectives by functional area of responsibility, as important to your management team as they are to you? If not, why not?

Managing Your Cash and Budget

One of the best ways to raise cash is not to spend the cash you already have in the bank. As the CEO you get to set an example for everyone and develop an operating and spending culture that every employee in the company will follow, now and in the future. Your team is observing your actions all the time. Remember people will follow what you do more than what you say. Here are some things to think about:

- If you fly first class, I would not consider making an investment in your company regardless of what its ultimate potential might be. That is just my perspective on such fundamental internal-cultural issues. Many other investors in our industry share my position on this matter. Some companies allow business class on long trips, and sometimes this might makes sense. However, when I was flying with a group, I would always fly coach to send a message. Actually, I always flew coach simply because it was part of our culture. If five people are flying coach to Asia or Europe, and the difference in fare between coach and business class is $5K, then you just saved the company $25K, which sends a message that will last much longer than the trip.
- If at an early start-up stage you are spending cash to enjoy an office or lab environment that presents a good image, think again. It is way too early in your business plan for such creature comforts. You can have a beautiful lab or office after you start

generating a profit. What you need now is something low budget but highly functional to get the job done.

- Encourage your team members to protect valuable cash, and acknowledge their achievements when they find better prices or less costly alternatives.

- Create an hour glass mind-set: there is only so much sand (or cash) in your bank account, and the faster you spend it, the sooner you run out of cash.

- More importantly, separate the frills and the creature comforts from the substantive issues that contribute to your tactical and strategic goals. If you say you are going to apply the savings on airfare or something else to purchase a new piece of badly needed diagnostic equipment for the lab or clinical supplies for a study, it comes home to all and is readily accepted. You don't need to scare people or make them feel uncomfortable. You just need to articulate the difference between creature comfort spending and investing precious cash wisely.

- Now, on the other hand, invest what is required to buy the very best equipment needed to achieve success, or to expand a clinical study to increase its success, and in general carefully and willingly fund those items that directly contribute to the achievement of the strategic goals and objectives.

- Make budgeting an important requirement for your direct reports, but only if you are really going to take advantage of a routinely updated budget. Again, actions speak louder than words, and the company culture begins with you.

Developing Your Strategic Plan

In chapter 4 we discussed setting the long-term business strategy and current-year tactical operating objectives. We also discussed methods for a CEO to accomplish these important planning matters for the company. In this section we are going to presume those goals and objectives have been set, and now it is time to develop the business plan. First let's recognize that a budget is just the quantification of the operating objectives for the next planning year. Likewise, the strategic business plan is just the quantification of the stated strategic business goals, whether for a thousand days or some other duration. Many CEOs and CFOs find it useful to forecast the first year of the plan by month, and the second and third year by quarter. This clearly puts more emphasis on year 1.

So now you have a useful set of strategic goals and tactical objectives (for year 1 of the plan), and you are ready to develop the business plan. Done properly and updated often, this plan can serve as next year's budget as well as the long-term (thousand-day) business plan. Let's quantify each of the key items one at a time.

Key Assumptions

The first section is a list of your key strategic goals and then your tactical operating objectives for the first full year of the plan. The first time you do make this list, it will be the most difficult thing to do, but you will get better at this over time.

Understanding the Components of an Income Statement

Revenues
Development Company

You are either a development company with no product revenues or a marketing company. You need to be thinking about possible licensing agreements over the next thousand days, or service/contract revenues, or any other form of revenue, such as a government grant or something else. Quantify these items, estimate a time frame, and before you know it, you have a revenue forecast for a development company.

Product Sales / Service Revenue Company

If you are forecasting product or revenue sales, first consider that it is important that you plan both dollars and units; that means you also have to forecast sales price. Furthermore, recognize that you may be distributing to more than one class of trade, so you need to be thinking about a revenue forecast that is prepared first by class of trade and then they within each class of trade of forecast by units and unit sales prices extending to sales dollars by each unit within each class of trade category. price by that class of trade and dollars. This way, you now have the information that you need to do a cost-of-sales budget and to forecast production requirements. The important thing is to do this projection correctly the first time and establish it as a useful tool for later use. Once your build your planning models, it will become easier to develop additional levels by product group or code. Developing your business plan in such a way allows this planning exercise to serve as both a thousand-day plan and a budget. If you use one model, your team will be able to update the plan periodically with less effort than if you built it from scratch each time. Your chief financial officer or controller or the like should be able to build the financial planning model to support the group effort.

Cost of Sales / Goods Sold

Your revenue forecast was developed by product, so your cost of sales also needs to be developed by product. You have the cost of sales and the cost of goods sold, and the difference between the two is distribution costs, other costs of sales, royalties, and other items that may be specific to your company.

Gross Profit

This item is normally net sales less the cost of goods sold. However, your revenue forecast right now is gross sales, not net sales. At this point you estimate sales returns and allowances, product returns, special off-invoice promotions, and your standard early-payment discount on invoices. Once you can determine net sales, subtract the total cost of goods sold from net sales to get gross profit. It is always useful to also show gross profit in each period of planning as a percentage of net sales.

Operating Expenses

These are expenses for items that are not directly associated with a product unit cost or an invoice or sale price. They normally include the following:

General and administrative expenses: Administrative staff, accounting, legal, auditing, patents and trademarks, investor relations, board and committee expenses, insurance, and so on.

Other Organizational Issues to Consider

Employees: First begin with an employee head count to include full-time, part-time, and seasonal employees. Add employee costs to include company-incurred payroll taxes, employee benefits, and all other employee-related costs. These employee expenses should be budgeted within the function where the employees work, not as an administrative cost.

Development programs: Develop your company budget by development program involving the direct (nonemployee) costs for each. It is useful to allocate the percentage of time required by each of the development team members to each project with time reconciliation at the end.

Clinical studies: Each study requires a separate plan to reflect primary and secondary end points, enrollment, power calculation issues, cost per patient, physician cost per patient, labs, clinical supplies, statistics, protocol development, site setup and audits, data control and collection, and data management, for example.

Marketing: First define each promotional program/objective, and then budget for it along with the timing of those activities. Plan for personnel, new head count, meetings, and promotion events, and so on as per the marketing plan. Obviously this applies only to a company that is marketing a product. However, this may involve a trade and/or scientific meeting for the purpose of licensing or partnering technology, so consider this last item as either a promotional item or a development cost item.

Sales: If you have a sales force, list the staff, travel, cars, samples, training, meetings, sales materials/aids, and all items associated with supporting a field sales force.

Note: Very often a company will combine R&D and clinical and regulatory affairs. This is an individual choice depending on your particular company. The important issue is that these categories match fairly well with how you run and organize your business, so keep it simple and easy to work with.

Investor Relations

As you prepare to go public, you need to be thinking about a more formalized investor relations program. Up until now you might have had a small list of large private investors that are typically more involved with the company that public shareholders and therefore informed. With a public IPO, you add what could be thousands of new shareholders. You need a communications mechanism, a website, periodic conference calls, investor meetings and forums where management presents to investors, annual reports, and annual shareholder meetings, to name a few. You also need this function to be managed by a person with the appropriate skills. Also, your financial team will be much more involved in submitting 10-Q reports to the SEC, annual proxy statements, board and committee meeting minutes and communications, periodic complaints from shareholders, NASDAQ or other exchange listing and reporting issues, and payments, to name a few. This is all part of the burden and cost of being a public company.

Take away items

- Define your business strategy and set the culture of your company in the very beginning and stick with it. Set the example for everything.
- If you have never been in general management (CEO, President, General Manager positions) you need to understand that you

will have many new functions that need to be managed by good people.

- Understand that it is your job to orchestrate all the moving parts of this company. You are the maestro of this orchestra.
- As the CEO you have bottom line responsibility and will be accountable to your board and your shareholders at all times
- Understand that going forward that you need to deliver what it is you said you were going to deliver.
- Be truthful and timely with all information to your investors, and be especially truthful and timely with bad news. Investors understand that they took risk but what they will never tolerate is being misled. Build trust early with your investors and maintain that trust throughout your journey.

CHAPTER 6

BUILDING YOUR EXECUTIVE TEAM

Recruit the very best team of operating executives you can find, then challenge, grow and motivate them to perform and achieve levels they never thought possible

You have the important responsibility of defining the structure of your management team and then recruiting the best talent you can find to work for you. You can never have too good of a team. The best team wins and it starts at the top with the CEO, the head coach.

In this chapter the strategy for team formation will be discussed, particularly how it applies to your chosen business strategy. The skills set of your team will be quite different if you are a technology company that licenses to commercial partners, vs. a fully integrated operating company that directly manufactures and sells it product to customers. It is important to think carefully about the long-term skill sets of your new key executive positions so that the person you hire initially, also has the skill sets needed a few years later when the organization has a different set of challenges. As we discussed, in order to make the best decision on the recruitment and selection of talent for key positions it is first important to understand the short- and long-term challenges of those positions. This chapter is intended to shed some light on the broader timeline needs of recruiting and job challenges in an effort to provide some food for thought on a broader number of functional challenges.

What is the Normal Source of the CEO Talent Pool?

Life science development companies are founded by CEO/entrepreneurs that often come from either one of two career pathways, that is technical or business.

Technical pathway. Often the CEO is an accomplished scientist with a background in research, development, or clinical research. The technical CEO may come from an educational institution, a hospital, a private or government research center, or a corporation. He/she may have a Masters degree, a PhD, or an MD. Often technical CEO's have extreme technical talent and possess that great idea. It is not unusual for the technical CEO to have little business experience and/or management experience outside of their technical field of expertise.

Business pathway. Often the CEO may have an accomplished background that may include one or more disciplines such as sales and marketing, business development, partnering, investment banking, finance, or law. The business CEO may often come from a successful career at another large or small corporation. He/she may have a business degree, a science degree, perhaps an M.B.A (Masters of Business Administration) degree and often comes with experience in launching products, negotiating business deals, and possibly raising capital.

The star CEO. From the above you can see that if you could combine the talents of the Technical and Business CEO you would have the perfect background of a Life Science CEO. Now if that CEO also ran and successfully exited other startups that have made his/her investors buckets of money then you have the star CEO. Star CEO's do exist, are aggressively sought after, but they are few and far between, so we plan for the normal CEO recruitment.

The Technical CEO is expected to be competent and excel on the technical side but must learn to excel on the business side. On the other hand the Business CEO is expected to be competent and excel on the business side and must learn to excel on the technical side. To manage your company properly and also to be successful in raising capital, you need to be knowledgeable and fully conversant in both areas.

You learn by asking questions to the high quality employees, advisors and board members you recruit. Asking questions and getting intelligent answers from such an expert talent pool allows you to learn important matters at a level of detail you have not been exposed to before. Sometimes you just don't know what you don't know, so surround yourself with people that have the answers. Understand the objectives of those new functions and challenges, why they are important, what resources are needed to address them, and what are the many things that can go wrong along the way. Never be afraid to ask questions. No CEO knows every little detail of every project within the company because that is simply impossible. I always have lots of questions and the more questions I ask the better I get at it. Everyone tends to respect a good relentless questioner and they come better prepared to discuss important matters with you as the CEO. Questions also show your executive team that you are really paying attention to what they are recommending, want to learn more to support the recommendation, and want to be informed on any progress on this matter. The successful CEO must be able to understand and execute both the technical and business disciplines well from a high level. It is perfectly normal for you to build a team that compliments your skill set. Therefore, the technical CEO is going to recruit high quality business executives earlier in his/her recruiting cycle, and the business CEO is going to recruit high quality technical executives earlier in his/her recruiting cycle. The CEO from either background should always keep in mind that it is often better to hire a part-time high quality, experienced consultant to handle certain functions than hire a less experienced full-time executive, or manager, for a certain position that may not have the full complement of talents and experiences for the long term development of the company. The number of people you manage is not important. What matters is that you are developing great technology in the best way possible, with the best advice available.

CEO Backgrounds. Your industry is unique in that start-up companies operate for years without revenues and spend huge amounts of capital in order to obtain product approval. Very few industries have this profile. CEO's are recruited with varying levels of management experience and tend to gain experience over time. Often CEO's without any prior general management experience are recruited for the CEO position either because they are the scientist behind that great idea, or they were a rainmaker with other companies on the business side. In this book we spend a little more time on management issues because I believe it is so important to achieving your dream. Yes, while some of these issues may pertain to small company growth companies in general. It is my belief that management is particularly important in your industry where many technical people have limited management and administrative experience. Likewise many business executives have excellent sales or other business experience, but little general management or technical management experience. A CEO is a general manager involved and ultimately responsible for every function in the company, not just a few. The CEO job is uniquely multi-dimensional by design. Therefore it is quite different from being in charge of one-dimensional functions like product development, clinical research, sales, marketing, or manufacturing. There is no job in the company similar to the CEO job. You now have many functions and dimensions to manage and integrate to successful achieve your business plan objective, not one. In general your development companies are small in terms of employee count initially with fewer moving parts that a full operating company that has to deal with sales and manufacturing on a daily basis. However, a successful CEO is going to want to implement efficient management systems and processes from the beginning to ensure long-term product success and a favorable exit. Hopefully, much of the material in this chapter will help prevent some problems and offer a few solutions to complex management challenges.

Human Resource Planning

People develop products and technologies—machines and patents do not. Your employees are one of your most valuable company assets; please never forget that. Employees are not expenses walking into the building every day. Instead your employees are opportunities to achieve your company's long- and short-term goals. Embrace your employees and encourage them to contribute their best to the company. In the process build the best team at all management levels to improve your chances for success. Finally, invest in succession planning to cull the weak and promote those that are ready for higher levels of responsibility. In a way a management team is only as strong as its weakest link. You should always keep this in mind and either strengthen that weak link or replace it.

Are you the right person for the CEO position?

It all starts at the top, and a good organization begins with the right CEO. Now, it is important for you to be honest with yourself. Are you the best executive for the CEO position going forward or just initially? The challenges and skill sets that a CEO will change from the early start up period, to the middle development period, to the end phase commercial period. Some CEO's take the full journey from start-up to exit, take only part of the journey. You are doing this to cause that great idea to come to fruition, and most likely you are interested in being financially rewarded for that contribution. Perhaps at the end of this book, you will revisit this suggestion. If you are not the best person for the CEO position at all times, then you should plan for the change. Keep in mind that it would be best for any new CEO to build his/her own team to his/her satisfaction rather than you doing it for him/her. Therefore, if you anticipate a CEO change, it is best to do it sooner than later, before you start recruiting senior-level executives. Ego can, and always does, get in the way. The important thing is that you receive a fair level of equity for starting the company and contributing the intellectual property, and are always properly recognized for what you do. Over time, that special something will happen that you will get credit for, and the value of your shares should increase and you should benefit handsomely if the company is successful. If another person is more qualified to be the CEO of your company, you really should consider the change if you want long-term developmental and financial success to be achieved. This decision is best coming from you early, especially if you suspect others are already thinking about it. If so, negotiate the change with your board to provide yourself the best financial advantage while still remaining active in a quality position with the company that is more in your comfort zone. Having the right CEO on board is extremely important in funding.

Line and Staff Functions. During my career I had the opportunity to have responsible positions in both line and staff functions. Both are necessary and if managed properly you have the opportunity as CEO to optimize the efficiency of your company by using both functions effectively. Line function executives are busy driving the key objectives to enable the company to grow and prosper. Staff function executives have a duel role, that is, to make the administrative activities of a line executive easier so as to enable that executive to focus on line functions that drive the growth of the business, while at the same time performing other functions and services that support the analysis of activities supporting the CEO and all executives. For example, a CFO should develop budgeting systems, techniques, and schedules that make the budgeting process for the managers of that executive easier and more meaningful to their own department planning. There should be a single planning concept not two plans that might involve one for the line function and one for the CEO. The HR functions should be proactive by initiating recruiting activity with the line executive even prior to the CEO/Board job approval. The job description and the background and requirements can come from discussion with the HR and Line executive early in the process so that when the job position is approved the recruiting can be executed in less time, therefore, supporting the line objectives. In general, the CEO must encourage the line executives and the staff executives to work together using the expertise of either party to meet the needs of the business. It is simply efficient and it saves cycle time enabling needed new hires to actually come on board sooner than later. As you know recruiting takes time.

The HR Executive

Planning for the growth and development of the HR (human resources) team is a critical company objective. The team you begin with will most likely not be the team you have two or four years later or more. When you are ready and able to expand your team, it makes sense to recruit a seasoned human resource professional to help you build your team, someone who has successfully done this in the past. This person should have outstanding recruitment skills, especially at the senior level, and good knowledge of employee benefits and hiring and termination procedures. This person should be elevated to be one of your direct reports and senior enough to even help you with your own direct reports from time to time. You want HR to run smoothly, with a steady hand, and not bring a crisis or a lawsuit to your attention too often.

If you are able to recruit a high-quality HR executive, you will find that this person will serve as a good company culture consultant, be a good sounding board on people issues, serve you extremely well with compensation issues in board interactions, help you build and fix your team's structures at all levels, administer your benefits plans and policies without taking time away from your line executives, support succession planning, and generally be a good advisor to you personally on what you are doing wrong or right as a leader. When you hit the level of the last point, you know you have a good person. You will be able to discuss certain people issues with your HR executive that may not be appropriate to discuss with other executives. At the same time it is useful to have someone tell you what you could occasionally be doing better to be a better leader or to deal with an issue that may not be aware of. So the right HR executive, at the right time, can substantially contribute to your growth spurt by enabling the line executives to spend more time on working with their respective teams to achieve the important operating objectives. Also, in the event you need to downsize or you merge with another company, this person will be invaluable, so look at this position in a broader, strategic sense instead of just recruiter.

Recruiting

Executive Recruiters

My experiences with using the services of executive recruiters to fill some of my key executive positions have been very good. Recruiters may appear to be expensive, but it is even more expensive to make the wrong choice or to take too long or never really fill the job and fail to execute your strategic plan. Finding the best recruiters becomes your initial challenge, and then that recruiter will work with you to help you define the kind of person you really want for your open executive positions. Furthermore, the recruiter will focus on the objective of filling those key executive slots you need filled and most likely will get it done sooner and better than if you did it yourself. By recruiting high-quality executives in a timely fashion, you are executing your goal of building a great management team to drive your strategic business plan.

Defining the Position

You are in a technology industry that requires a specialized level of educational skill for most positions. You want not just any chemist but a highly skilled organic chemist, or high-volume packaging supervisor, or a skilled plant-cost accountant, or a protein-production technician with very narrow or specialized skills in this area. The first step in recruiting is defining precisely the kinds of skills needed for this new position. Now clearly you don't hire someone for just one position but instead look at him/her as potentially a good employee with growth potential in other areas. However, it's best to get the first position right and hire the very best employee that also has potential in other areas. By narrowing the skill set and the focus of recruiting, your recruiting effort becomes more efficient. Also, be very specific about desired prior work experience as well as education and other factors that are relevant to this new position. Recruiting can be expensive, so by doing your homework and organizing your thoughts, you and your executive team are enabling your HR function to do the best job it can and speed up the recruiting process.

Interviewing

Initial screening should take place with a group of candidates that you believe sufficiently meet the key requirements. You may talk on the phone with five good prospects out of fifteen applicants, and you may invite only two to three candidates for a face-to-face interview with management. Make sure you are ready for the interviews and candidates when they come. I have always had the recruiting policy that if a new position reports to one of my direct reports, then I want to see the candidates before a final hiring decision. I don't need to see them all, but in the event my executive leaves for any reason, this new employee is now my problem or opportunity, and I want to be comfortable with him/her.

Making the Job Offer

We live in a litigious society. You would be surprised at how many employee-employer conflicts begin at the hiring stage. Every employee should be provided a properly written offer of employment, even temporary and part-time employees.

Nonexecutive employees: The offer of employment should describe the duties and responsibilities of the job being offered, the supervisor, the effective date of employment, the hours and days of work, and the hourly or salary compensation. If there are benefits involved (such as group medical insurance), then the benefits should be stated and details and/or brochures of the plan provided. If the job is eligible for bonus or vacation pay, it should be stated. Any special requirements of the job or weekly schedules need to be stated in the letter. The job may be temporary, and if so, that fact should be clearly stated to avoid confusion. Finally, the offer should be dated and signed by a company official and the new employee. Disputes with employees arise when there is ambiguity in compensation, responsibilities, reporting relationships, and longevity of the position. A properly worded employment letter will eliminate most of these disputes, and you will show the employee that the company is organized in the way it handles its employees.

Executives: For executives, the job offer may be more involved and may include termination provisions with termination for cause or no cause language, compensation, and other items that may be specific to a particular position or individual. Compensation issues with executives may involve salary, bonus, equity incentives, benefits, and so on, so it gets more complicated, which is why it is best to be clear on these matters up front. This protects the company from litigation in the case that executive needs to be terminated later. Leaving these matters open forces unpleasant compensation issues at a time of stress for both sides.

The CEO: Every board must have the right to terminate the CEO at will for the benefit of all shareholders if it feels that is appropriate. There should always be an employment agreement, and this employment agreement should describe the duties and responsibilities of the CEO position, the initial compensation, bonus plans, equity incentives, and employee benefits, as it does for other executives. It is very important that the agreement have a termination section and that termination be described fully under "cause" or "no cause" conditions. Often the severance agreements are different for cause or no cause. For example, if the CEO was convicted of crime, he/she may not be provided any severance pay, and all incentive programs might be impacted in various ways. There may be no vacation pay or medical benefits provided. On the other hand, if the board felt it had to make a change to get a more experienced/qualified CEO, the severance package most likely would be more generous, if immediate termination occurred. The contract should state what those compensation matters are relative to salary continuance, bonus payments, equity incentive vesting, employee benefits, and so on. The typical CEO understands that he/she serves at the pleasure of the board of directors at all times and that if his/her removal is arbitrary, the change is not punitive and allows the executive time and ability to seek a similar position somewhere else.

Performance Evaluations
This important management function is rarely executed well. Thus, many of these programs are quickly determined to be a waste of time by

some people. Normally, performance evaluations are done once a year. They are prepared in writing by the direct supervisor and verbally presented to the employee. The process is fine, but the problem is that we too often, for reasons of political correctness or fear of litigation, do not discuss the real issues. If this is a program you cannot perform properly, then stop doing it until you can. However, you should be counseling your direct reports on an ongoing basis during the year, one issue at a time. Remember you and every one of your executives and managers are leaders and coaches. Yes, you are their coach; they need to hear from you about what and how you do your job, and this should be a positive communication process. You will find that you cannot really change people, but you can modify their behavior, especially as it pertains to the job environment. Whether you conduct performance reviews formally or informally, it is important that you at least do one of them well.

Human Resource Policies

There will be a time where it becomes necessary to have formal company policies. Company policies may initially include the following:

- Employee benefits (group medical, disability, life insurance, etc.)
- Vacation policies
- Expense reporting guidelines/procedures
- Retirement plans

Your HR executive is responsible for initially drafting these plans and reviewing them with you, your team, and the board. All of this will eventually lead to a board-approved benefits plan. The CEO and HR team will be responsible for administering the plan consistently to all employees.

Finance and Accounting

Properly using your staff teams, such as HR and finance, to support the line functions can reap big rewards in the long run. Like everything, it starts with recruiting the best people that can do what is needed and then grow with the company and/or help drive its growth.

The financial executive function contributes to the development and growth of the company in several ways:

- Routine finance controls and procedures to meet minimum reporting requirements
- Financial reporting
- Asset-protection programs
- Budgeting to include the quantification of the business goals and objectives
- Personal support to all line executives with regard to their more demanding budgeting needs
- Presentation of / support for the annual budget, any updates, and the strategic plan for management and board review
- Driving the capital-formation plan and all related activities at all levels
- Expense-improvement programs
- Strategic business plan preparation/maintenance
- Investor interactions, updating materials, periodic conference calls and meetings
- Financial consulting to the CEO and executive team
- Board of director support for meetings and presentations, and if a formal corporate legal secretary is not part of the team, then the normal board-related corporate secretary functions with regard to minutes, shareholder meetings, filings, and so on

Operations/Manufacturing

For the purpose of this discussion, the operations/manufacturing function is falls under a wide umbrella to include the following:

- Facilities management
- Materials procurement

- Product development
- Engineering
- Production planning
- Manufacturing
- Maintenance
- Safety and OSHA programs
- Packaging
- Warehousing
- Inventory control
- Distribution
- Grounds and waste management
- Quality control

This is an executive position that will be broader or narrower depending on the business strategy of the company.

Fully Integrated Marketing Companies

This business strategy requires a full-service operations executive that has broad and deep operations experience to support the growth of your business. With this business strategy, the operations function is key component of your business on a daily basis. It is best to recruit a high-quality executive for this position as early as your funding and progress will allow.

Licensing/Partnering Companies

This business strategy requires high-quality operations support but in a more narrow, intermittent way. You will need to conduct some level of product development that may include formulation, stability, packaging, and possibly sterility, and you may have a need to produce GMP clinical supplies to support your partnering efforts. You will also need to carefully document procedures, formulas, and GMP processes and batch records for partner review. While you will not be running production daily or distributing finished goods, it is extremely important that what you do with regard to the above functions you do in a high-quality manner. The prospective corporate partners you will be speaking with, and hopefully negotiating with in the future, will require this. Your failure to deliver in a quality manner will directly impact the licensing terms you will be able to negotiate with these prospective partners. Simply put, they will expect you to conduct the above activities at a level of quality similar to their own internal standards.

Now, you can staff this team with someone who can learn all this part time, and many companies do. However, what I would rather see you do is to retain a high-quality part-time executive to drive the execution of these functions for you so that the function meets the quality standards of your corporate-partner prospects. This person may also be helpful in later representing your company with you in any partnering discussions, giving the partner confidence in the quality of the work, your team, and you. When corporate partners begin their due diligence, they bring in skilled operations professionals who will quickly determine that your operations trainee is just that, and the red flags will go up in the first five minutes of the meeting. Always recruit quality and experienced talent for a key function as it really is cheaper in the long run in terms of greater achievement, fewer mistakes, more reliability, higher levels of creditability with partners and investors, and minimal licensing revenue discounting due to partner concerns.

Sales and Marketing

This section applies to those companies that aspire to be a fully integrated operating company and manage their own sales and marketing functions as they sell product they manufacture, directly to their customer bases. In this section I combine marketing functions with the sales function. In most companies both functions report to one executive. Sales and marketing are two different functions, but with a common purpose, which causes most organizations to structure them as one integrated unit. Some companies go the additional step and place marketing and sales, and operations under one executive, often referred to as a chief operations officer (COO).

Depending on the industry, the pool of talent in marketing and sales involves different sources.

Consumer Products Companies
Marketing

The marketing team comprises the "Madison Avenue" types that have been trained in marketing concepts in the best of schools, have relevant experience, and understand market research, media, social networking systems, and many of the tools and programs that make for a well-crafted marketing plan. A marketing team is concerned with budgeting, pricing, product costs, promotional costs, gross profit, and competitive market analysis. Often your marketing team will be organized in a brand-management structure with one brand manager/director directing the marketing programs of a particular product or product line. Several of these brand managers constitute a brand-marketing department, which is responsible for preparing and justifying a substantial spending budget to grow and/or defend the brand. Brand managers, with executive approval, determine the selection and the spending priorities for a particular brand.

Sales

Consumer products involve various sales channels, including chain drug stores (Walgreens, CVS), mass merchandising chains (Wal-Mart, Target), and e-commerce venues (Amazon.com). Sales professionals that have extensive exposure usually develop the sales team. Establishing quality and profitable relationships with large, powerful retail chains is a task that depends on the talent and experience of your sales team. Once you have established such distribution agreements, you have to carefully and diligently manage the relationships with support for all the accountability and promotional programs that impact individual stores and their operations.

Rx Drug / Medical Device / Biologics Companies
Personnel

The marketing and sales functions are much more closely aligned in the prescription life science industry. Often field sales professions will migrate to marketing positions and vice versa. This is a very healthy development process that helps build the breadth and depth of experience of those involved in such programs. Many future executives in marketing and sales are former participants of such programs.

Prescriptions

Field sales representatives in your industry have the objective of getting the physicians serviced within that representative's call universe or territory to write prescriptions. Sales representatives do a number of things to make that happen, but in the end you cannot sell any prescription product without a prescription from a physician. The requirement for a prescription uniquely defines our industry and thus is the basis for our sales and marketing structures and programs.

When a sales representative meets with a physician, it is his/her responsibility to first understand his/her own products, second to understand his/her competitors and their products in a particular category, and third to know something about that physician's practice and the type of medical conditions he/she treats routinely.

Physicians are very busy and see many patients with various ailments. They prescribe many drugs (or devices or biologics), so there is much to remember. For the purpose of this section, I will speak to pharmaceuticals, but the same principles apply to medical devices and biological products. Physicians are human too, and to stay at the top of their game and treat and prescribe products that are the very best choice for a particular patient, they must focus on a few drugs in each category. It is not unusual for a physician to use three drugs routinely for a particular indication. Often his/her number one product choice represents 50 percent of the total prescriptions he/she writes, the number two choice 25 percent, and the number three choice about 15 percent. The 10 percent remaining can be all over the place and may be driven by price, patient preferences, and medical-reimbursement issues. What causes a physician to make the above choices has everything to do with the efficacy profile, the safety profile, and the patient's tolerance profile or primary treatment needs. A physician would love to use one drug for every type of medical indication, the one with the best overall efficacy and safety profile as determined by the FDA-approved labeling. Side effects often drive a physician to use a second-choice or third-choice drug. His/her choices are all made for a reason and are generally not arbitrary. A successful sales representative knows that the objective is to convince the physician of the benefits of his/her product based on the approved labeling and other appropriate means of providing professional information. This is necessary with a product introduction when no drug experience in the field exists, and later after the drug has been in use for a while. You always want your product to be the first choice that a physician reaches for to treat a patient for a specific indication. That is how you build prescription levels and increase product sales.

FDA-Approved Product Labeling

The above section describes a basic process that occurs inside a physician's office. Labeling drives that process, which is why it is so important to obtain regulatory approval for efficacy superiority or increased patient tolerance and safety.   In you industry it is illegal to discuss product uses and claim that have not been approved by the FDA. You may appreciate how a superior efficacy claim for a drug in a particular indication might enable a representative to convince physicians to use this new product as their first choice in all their patients. It usually does not happen that way, and physicians will usually go slowly and write more prescriptions, as they are convinced from patient reports that it has superior efficacy and lower safety issues. This takes time, but the labeling gives the representative in the field the ammunition to challenge and achieve the number one position with the highest prescription level.   What can ruin a promising product is an inferior or a restricted safety profile. This is also in the labeling, and if the company rep does not bring this up, the physician may find it out on his/her own. However for sure, the physician will hear all the negatives from the competing company's representative, who is in the physician's waiting room, waiting for your sales representative to leave. Labeling is very public, and the fortunes of worldwide drug/product sales levels depend dramatically on labeling for efficacy and safety. Understand that the competitive relationship of these factors is what eventually causes a change in a physician's prescribing behavior, often leading to prescription growth and higher sales.

Price, and more importantly medical reimbursement, can and does impact prescription choice on occasion. A sales representative may do all that is necessary to convince a physician to write that prescription only to have the patient ask for a different product that his/her insurance company will pay for instead of that expensive new drug. That is just the way it is. Eventually the insurance company may reimburse for the new drug, so you still may see the results, but only later.

Business Development

Licensing, in and out, and corporate partnering may be your chosen business strategy. A business-development function involves what can be described as sales activities combined with due diligence disclosure and finally negotiations. A successful business-development executive understands the product-development process, has the skills to work well with development and scientific staff, knows the value of intellectual property, and has a good sense of how partnering and licensing contracts should be developed for maximum financial benefit. In a small company, the CEO, supported by one or two members of the team, often handles this function. However, if the business strategy of your company is primarily to partner products and technologies, it is best to have a dedicated business-development professional on your executive team. This executive position should report to the CEO and needs to work closely with all line functions in concert with the plans set by the CEO. Keep in mind that this position essentially drives the commercial revenue stream and the ultimate valuation of the company. Therefore, the position should be filled by someone very experienced and capable for best results.

Research and Development

Just as it makes sense to put sales and marketing under one executive, the same is true for R&D (research and development). Research and drug/device/biologics development have separate objectives and require difference skill sets, but collectively the two groups have a common purpose and require close coordination and integration. For the purposes of this discussion, R&D includes research, development, clinical research, and regulatory affairs. This is another functional area that has been described in a number of books by itself. In this book I will cover the surface issues and speak more of the bigger picture and how to manage the overall process.

By their very nature, research programs focus on long-term discoveries and opportunities. If the opportunity happens to be a short-term opportunity, such as a product-line extension, it would not be managed within the research group.

Research

This function is often discovery research and involves the discovery and very early screening and testing of leads within standard or newly developed predictive efficacy models. Depending on the mission of your company, research can involve a wide variety of challenges. Many PhDs staff the research functions, and very often the teams with the highest level of talent produce the most-promising compounds for development. The research team members must be deeply aware of the global research being performed in their respective areas of discovery. It is useful for them to attend the appropriate scientific meetings and network with many of their counterparts. The research team is encouraged to patent and then publish, bringing forward the best new mechanisms of action, compounds, techniques, and other discoveries that will enable the company to bring forward the very best in medical therapies. In drug development we often begin with a molecule, so it is often chemical synthesis, or alternatively building cell lines, or another means of producing research material that enables the team to begin the process by first working with promising material.

It is important that the research team, like all other critical functions, has a defined mission and a set of priorities. It is important that the research programs test many prospective product candidates and objectively separate the promising ones from the less promising. The promising candidates, after further screening, will move on to the development team for more traditional, rigorous development. The research director has the responsibility to define this in collaboration with the research team and then use that defined program to justify staffing and spending going forward. Every functional group in the company can and should be held accountable, and research is no exception. There needs to be a focus, and there need to be goals to file patents, publish papers, attend scientific meetings, and in general continue the professional development of the scientific team for the benefit of the company. In a small company, this may be a very limited operation if it even exists, while in a larger company, it may a very substantive operation. Regardless, goals and even short-term objectives can and should be articulated and communicated. In a small company, it is not unusual for the discovery arm to be closely connected with a university.

University Collaborations

There is a great deal of talent and technology opportunity available with university research groups. These groups may or may not be funded or supplemented in some way with government organizations. It is very important that a proper, formal technology-development agreement be put in place with any third parties. These agreements often require supplemental funding and collaborative goals and activities, and define compensation to the institution in the form of royalties and perhaps other payments. There are no standard forms for such agreements, and it is best to retain a professional that has negotiated such agreements in the past to assist your company. Be mindful that an agreement with a university for one of your lead compounds that might eventually be licensed to a Big Pharma company will require a much higher level of scrutiny by Big Pharma. In the end, if the terms are unacceptable, this university agreement, which might have been signed years ago, could become an albatross for the company, or its best asset. The patent quality and global patent coverage are also very important to a prospective partner. If the university has chosen to patent only US rights, and often it has, this can be determined to be a deal breaker for a global commercialization firm. How you configure and negotiate these early university agreements will ultimately impact your commercialization potential. Therefore, use the services of a seasoned professional to assist you with this transaction.

Animal Testing

While this function is a subject of controversy for some, understand that animal testing is an integral part of drug development and is required by the FDA to ensure the safety of pharmaceuticals in humans. Over the years many specific and refined animal models have been developed; they tend to be good predictors of how certain candidates may impact human organs such as the heart, skin, kidneys, and liver. Animal testing produces incredibly valuable information to help understand dosing levels, ADME (absorption, distribution, metabolism, excretion) functions, efficacy, and toxicity. It is important that every company sponsor—that is, the company developing the product—know the lowest and highest dose that achieve efficacy and also the lowest which toxicity is observed and results in animal sacrifice. This critically valuable information will later be used to determine the initial dose and dosing ranges in a phase I safety clinical trial. These tests are performed with utmost care and concern for the testing animals through final sacrifice. The need for animal testing reduces human deaths and safety problems and enables enable safe, life-saving therapies to enter the market. Well-controlled, regulated animal testing programs are absolutely a necessary part of drug development, and are required by the FDA.

Product Development

The quality and effectiveness of all your teams that you recruit is critical. If you are a development company that licenses its products and technologies, it is especially important that you teams excel in this function. The development function will typically take early product leads passed on from research and move them through various development steps to determine their worthiness for continued development. Understand that many leads will enter the development process, with very few reaching FDA approval. Therefore, without throwing the baby out with the bathwater, it is important to be disciplined and terminate leads along the development pathway when it becomes clear that others have superior efficacy profiles or when safety issues warrant no further support for their continued development. This natural culling allows a development team with limited resources to continue to invest in the most-promising leads.

Companies in our industry may or may not have a need for dedicated research teams, or clinical teams, or marketing and sales teams, and so on, but most companies in our industry are involved with development at varying stages and levels. If you plan to license your leads or portions of your technology platform, your development effort will focus on the early stages of development, perhaps with limited clinical development. If your plan is to take a lead or leads to market, you face the full requirements of drug development from early leads through the clinical program, regulatory filing, and finally FDA-approved labeling. Clearly the latter business strategy will require the largest development group and will require the selection of outstanding executives and department heads to enable the development function to achieve success. Some of the development functions many smaller companies may require include the following:

- Formulation/dosing/administration: Is this lead administered orally, intravenously, intramuscular, transdermal, ocular, or mucosal? Is it dosed once a day, twice a day, or once a month?

- Stability and possibly sterility: Does it have a shelf life of five years, one year, one month? Does it need to be refrigerated or reconstituted?
- ADME (absorption, distribution, metabolism, excretion): This describes the disposition of a pharmaceutical compound within an organism (animal or man).

Product Development / GMP Clinical Supplies

In most R&D activities, a lead compound candidate is dosed in various ways that, for the most part, are based on the weight of the animal being tested. As a candidate successfully moves through the process and toward human clinical testing, a more uniform dose form needs to be developed. In our industry, and this is unique, a product that enters the clinic for human clinical testing must be manufactured according to GMP (good manufacturing practices) standards. This requirement often necessitates a substantial manufacturing investment at an early stage that in most other industries is delayed until the technology risk is lower. There are good reasons for this, the primary one being the testing of a consistently produced product so that the results of one study can be compared to another. This requirement is often a substantial funding challenge for the small development company. It is important to also point out that if the company wishes to partner this technology, the prospective partners also require high standards. They want those high standards for their own business decisions, and they are looking toward the scrutiny that they will encounter later with the various regulatory agencies. Some of the challenges in this area that need to be funded at this preclinical stage include the following, based on an example of a small-molecule chemical compound:

14. Chemical synthesis: A rigorous chemical-synthesis process needs to be finalized at a certain batch size level, perhaps ten kilograms at this stage. The batch size is important because it will be necessary to scale up to larger batch sizes later, and it is advisable not to scale up beyond ten times the previously validated batch size.
15. GMP (Good Manufacturing Practices) manufacturing: This refers to the process, procedures, controls, and batch records involved in consistently manufacturing one batch of the active ingredient. GMP

validation is a regulatory requirement that generally involves producing three consecutive and consistent GMP batches (active ingredient). If all three batches have been identically produced, and if their profiles are identical, then this is considered a validated manufacturing process. Again, this requires three consecutive batches, not three out of five. If your process and manufacturing methods are really well developed, then three consecutive successful batches will prove that. Again, this validation will be important to your prospective partners and the regulatory agencies and you need to do it properly to support your credibility.

16. Final dose form: To simplify this example, we will presume the final dose form is a tablet taken once a day, and the various dosages are five, ten, and fifteen milligrams. The team will need determine the shape of the pill, the color, coatings, and the binders and fillers necessary for the pill to retain its shape, color, and integrity for years in a plastic bottle.

17. Stability (shelf life): Long-term stability testing determines the shelf life of the pill, and this is an important issue for commercialization. These stability studies measure the effect of time, humidity, temperature, and other conditions that may be unique to this particular product. Five years from the date of manufacture is always a desirable outcome; a shorter shelf life could possibly create problems with distribution. Shelf lives of only one to two years are often problematic in the field.

18. Packaging: The package that the dosage form is stored in should use the same materials as the final package to make sure there is no variability in results.

Clinical

General
Preparation for Clinical Trials

Before a sponsor (the company) can even consider a human clinical trial, an investigational new drug (IND) application need to be filed with and accepted by the FDA. This regulatory submission package compiles all the animal data produced, with detailed information regarding mostly safety and efficacy in animals, if the latter is available. The package is extensive and includes a human clinical trial protocol recommended by the sponsor. It is also important to note that before clinical trials can begin, the company must have produced clinical supplies according to GMP compliance. The agency has the right to stop you from proceeding with this trial for a period, and can stop a sponsor from continuing any human clinical trial at any time. Once the review period of the IND has expired with no objections raised, you are free to begin your clinical program

There are three general phases to the human clinical development program, described in the following sections.

Phase I

This is the "first in man" study, and its primary purpose is to initial establish safety in humans. Understand that safety is never established until final FDA labeling and approval are granted. This study or these studies normally involve multiple ascending doses and may involve one or more doses per day. These studies are normally conducted using the safety data produced in animal models that will assist in determining high and low dose ranges for safety. For human safety reasons, the FDA will not allow a higher kilogram-dosage used in humans than has been previously tested in animal models. All human clinical trials are structured with the utmost care for the volunteers that participate in the study; however, the initial phase I study is always of particular concern until some human safety data has been established. There can be more than one phase I trial, and the sponsor anticipates that the previously conducted animal studies regarding safety will initially be confirmed in humans. The fact that phase I has completed and the sponsor has FDA approval to move on to phase II should never imply that all safety testing is complete. Safety testing never ends.

Phase II

This next clinical phase involves both safety and some level of efficacy. Patient volunteers diagnosed with the anticipated target indication of the candidate make up the human population of this study. Now staying within the safety parameters of the previous phase I safety trials, phase II testing attempts to determine efficacy in patients. Typically these studies start with a low dose and move higher to better assess efficacy in true patients. The initial phase II studies tend to involve smaller patient populations. Multiple phase II trials are the norm and are highly recommended to best position your phase III study investment. The phase II stage enables the sponsor the opportunity to better profile patients, dosages, and safety issues to determine whether there are any patterns worthy of further investigation. It is also a time to conduct additional studies with larger numbers of patients to better explore and understand previously observed relationship patterns of patient profiles (weight, age, condition, gender, race, etc.) that react differently, from both a safety and an efficacy perspective, involving lower or higher daily doses. This valuable knowledge is critical in designing the phase III pivotal trial program.

Note: I am always skeptical of small companies that conduct one simple phase I trial and one simple phase II trial and attempt to convince third parties that they have established safety and efficacy. Sorry, it is just not that simple!

Phase III

This is the most critical step in the clinical program and by far the most expensive. The objective at the end of the phase III program is to conduct human clinical trials that achieve statistically significant results regarding the primary end point of the trial as predefined in conference with the FDA. Usually two such studies of sufficient size are required to obtain FDA approval. If you achieve this result, most likely you are on your way to regulatory approval. If not, you just invested an enormous amount of capital with no return.

If your chosen business strategy is a development company that partners your programs, your clinical team most likely will be involved in phase I clinical trials and possibly phase II trials, but probably not phase III trials and regulatory approvals. This is an important issue with regard to staffing your clinical team. There are a number of quality third party clinical research firms that can perform phase I and phase II clinical trials.

Regulatory

We work in a regulated business, and everything we do pre- and post marketing remains under the scrutiny of one or more federal agencies at all times.

Let me just say this about regulatory responsibilities: If you are not committed to complying with regulations, then you are in the wrong business. Your partners do not need regulatory problems or challenges in obtaining approval for things that your company did. You need to convince them that you respect the regulatory process and have and will continue to maintain full compliance at all times. Remember that it is entirely possible that the approval your partner is attempting to achieve could be held up by something your company did five years ago. Everybody loses on something like this, so when your partner sends in a team of regulatory staff, they are often mostly concerned with making sure you performed the study properly and it will not adversely impact them with the FDA at a later date.

In a small company, it is very important that you have a quality regulatory point person that can provide guidance to you and your team and represent you in important due diligence meetings with prospective partners. If you hire a trainee, your partner will be concerned, and you should be also. Always have the best professionals on your team. It does not matter whether they are full-time employees or part-time consultants; the important issue is that they know what they are doing and do quality work for the company for internal and partnering use.

Phase IV: Post-approval Marketing Programs

This post approval program sequentially follows regulatory simply because it will not be executed until and after FDA approval is granted. Essentially a Phase IV program is a marketing support clinical program. Once FDA approval is granted, there are often reasons to generate competitive superiority data for marketing purposes. Studies are often conducted with the objective of a published paper or, better, an FDA-approved marketing claim. The former will be of interest to physicians, who can decide whether such information will change their prescribing habits; the latter gives the company the legal right to market and sell that claim to physicians and is always the best-case outcome.

Take Away Issues

- Remember that a team is like a chain, and a chain is only as strong as it weakest link
- You will be judged by the quality of the team you put in place.
- Always hire the very best person for every key position
- People develop products, people raise capital, people commercial technology at all levels. Your employees represent your greatest assets.

Once FDA approval is granted, there are often reasons to generate competitive superiority data for marketing purposes. Studies are often conducted with the objective of a published paper or, better, an FDA-approved marketing claim. The former will be of interest to physicians, who can decide whether such information will change their prescribing habits; the latter gives the company the legal right to market and sell that claim to physicians and is always the best-case outcome.

Intellectual Property Enhancements

Too many companies make the mistake of dropping their guard once their first patent is granted in the United States. Patents will drive the exit value of your business, and you must manage them and protect them at all times. Keep them current in everyone's thinking and planning with improved communication and exposure. Know that Big Pharma companies want patent protection in Europe and Asia, not only North America and not just the United States. Also, appreciate how important it is to continue to work your discovery to make sure you file additional continuations-in-part during the allowable period. Broaden, strengthen, and protect your intellectual property to the best of your ability.

Most small companies work with quality patent attorneys, and it is very important that you very clearly assign one of your executives the responsibility of managing intellectual property and all the associated internal communications demanded by such responsibility. Make sure you are personally involved with all key decisions regarding your company's intellectual property. The quality of your intellectual property estate has everything to do with your ability to close quality corporate partnerships and/or licensing agreements.

Take Away Issues

- How you manage your team and your company objectives has everything to do with your ultimate success.
- Remember that a team is like a chain and a chain is only as strong as it weakest link
- A CEO by definition must constantly multitask and deal with the problems and challenges involving multiple functions simultaneously.
- Hire the best team you can but remember leadership is a full-time job that one must exercise at all times

CHAPTER 7

ESTABLISHING STRATEGIC GOALS AND OBJECTIVES

Plan you work, then work your plan

I have always been supportive of good, thoughtful planning but have never been a big fan of the ten-year strategic business plan. The reason is simple: most people cannot reliably plan more than two to three years out, and I think most business executives would agree with me. Years 4 through 10 often wind up being a silly mathematical exercise with little value, so why do it? More importantly, don't rely on it.

What I have found to be more useful in lieu of a ten-year strategic business plan are the following two types of planning tools:

Thousand day plan. Consider a thousand-day business plan projection and take the time to plan the first twenty-four months as best as you can. The discipline of building this plan will strengthen your team, your relationship with your team, and the relationships between each of your executives. This plan and this process will allow you to communicate your plan more intelligently to your board with a strong level of confidence. This plan, once complete and approved, should be summarized for third-party consideration, and if it is well prepared, it should present you, your team, and your company favorably. One important operating/cultural benefit of such a planning process is the definition of the company's key strategic critical success factors. I have always found that if the board and management team can agree on such a list, making other decisions is easier as it provides an operating or moral compass to guide the company.

Technology Plans

- Lead program pipeline plan to the point of commercialization. This would be presented in a visual timeline, usually a Ghannt chart depicting the various pipeline programs over a period of years horizontally. The chart may present the later stage programs on top descending to the earliest research or pre-clinical programs in the pipeline. The first three years of this plan should tie in with the thousand-day financial projection plan.

- Long range therapeutic outlook plan. In pharmaceuticals it is necessary and strategically important to look way beyond today's current therapies and at the new discoveries and shifts in treatment that are on the horizon and for which a great deal of research is going on around the world. As you know, a basic research project is ten years away from market. Your scientific team needs to be looking out far enough to capture the trends and the new treatment categories, methods, chemical classes, and so on. My experience suggests that team members will embrace a meaningful planning exercise that is useful, and therefore meaningful, to them. If so, you have the basis for team coordination, executive task integration, budgets, personnel planning, capital items, and overall cash flow projections. What is more important is that this effort addresses the strategic direction of the market and the company, with the financial impact being initially of less importance. My experience suggests that this plan is best developed with a maximum of thought regarding intermediate and long-term trends, and a minimum of numbers and dollar projections. The long-term trends matter, and this scientific strategic therapeutic program plan should provide the board a meaningful guide to future therapies of tomorrow might be.

Embracing the Culture of Business Planning

If this process is successful, each executive will now have a reason to embrace the plan and allow the plan to become the basis for setting all company goals and all functional and departmental objectives within his/her area of responsibility. Such processes, if performed correctly, will enable all of the team to get in one boat to row together for a common purpose to achieve your collective business objectives.

Accepting/embracing a planning system: You might wish to begin this process in the early fall with the first planning year beginning in the following January. One thousand days is approximately 2.75 years, with the final quarter of year 3 being a time bonus. It is helpful to forecast the first year by month, and the second and third year by quarter. This way you essentially build your budget for next year as part of your thousand-day plan, and you are building a plan based on key long-term goals, critical success factors, short-term functional objectives, and subsequent departmental objectives by executive. When finished, the result is a complete planning model for multiple purposes. Build the model properly, and it will be much easier to complete the second time around. Also, take the time to update next year's annual budget once or twice during the year to keep all this current.

Management Team and Objectives

One of the most important challenges of any CEO is to define, recruit, build, and optimally manage a strong management team. Once it is built, it is the charge of the CEO to build a culture that enables that team to function efficiently and effectively, improving it constantly to coincide with the then-current strategic and tactical challenges of the company.

It is not possible to have a management team that is too good. It takes a great deal of talent on the part of the CEO to recruit and retain a quality management team. That task is easier said than done, but the ultimate success of the company depends on the quality of the management team and your ability to optimize the management team's contributions. Too often a management team is built based on friendship, family, trustworthiness, and loyalty. It is also important to have the best available executive in a given position at all times.

Setting Tactical Business Objectives

At the CEO level, you have to learn to manage other highly qualified executives in the form of vice presidents and get them all to work as one cohesive, integrated machine. This involves a certain level of management skill that not all CEOs have, particularly those in start-up companies. Very often this can be like herding cats, but despite the challenge, you need to get it done. Business plan requirements need to be set on both the strategic (goals) and tactical (objectives) levels. I have always found it useful to spend time developing strategic goals of the company in a meaningful manner with the full participation of the executive and senior management team charged with actually executing the plan. The CEO is the business leader and therefore has to lead this effort. Developing company plans and achieving business objectives are prime responsibilities of any CEO. Therefore, if the CEO cannot do this, then it is in the best interests of the company and shareholders for the board to appoint a CEO that can develop a meaningful business plan and execute it.

The plan begins by defining the mission and strategic goals of the company. This needs to be done in a serious, thoughtful manner. It is always useful to develop a plan that a management team can get its arms around in a time frame that is manageable, and achievable to those responsible for executing the plan. Often I present it as a thousand-day plan so it winds up being a plan for the next three calendar years. Most people can deal with a thousand-day plan, but they often lose interest beyond year 4. If you focus your team on the first two years of the thousand-day plan, with emphasis on year 1, and you will see a different response to the effort. If your senior executives cannot plan properly for the next two years, you need to recruit executives that can. Discuss this concept in the office to get the executive team thinking about it for a few days before setting a date for a one- to two-day offsite planning meeting for the top executive team only.

The Thousand-Day Plan

Primary purpose: First, it is useful that your board knows you are having this executive planning meeting and that you will report the results and recommendations to the board. Second, make sure you pick a private, quiet place so you and your team will be comfortable and will not be interrupted during these two days. Do not make the mistake of attempting to do this in the office. The primary purpose of this meeting is to define and develop goals for the thousand-day plan for the purpose of a presentation to the full board. Let your executives know up front that they will be involved in presenting their parts of the plan. Once they know this, it will surprise you to see how fast they begin to pay attention and contribute to the process. Peer pressure is always very powerful.

Secondary purpose: This is your opportunity to exhibit the leader within you. This is your team, your mission, your company, and your plan that you are going to recommend to your board. If you think you are the only CEO that has trouble getting his/her executives to cooperate with each other, think again. This problem exists everywhere, and it is your job to minimize it. The meeting provides you a chance to get the team to agree on a set of plans and disagree on others. In the end the team will sift it out and agree on a plan that works, if you stick with it and provide the necessary environment for teamwork. This is also an opportunity for the team members to bond on key business issues, in this case a set of plans and goals that they collectively will be responsible for. Take this opportunity to attempt to have some fun, as fun is also good for team building. If you do this right, the team will develop a set of company goals that make sense.

Then it is time to work on the functional goals of each executive and his/her respective team. This second part comes later and is extremely important for the overall integrity of the companywide plan. In some cases, it will become apparent to some team members for this first time that what they do, how they do it, and when they deliver it matters to another team executive. The synchronization of this entire plan by functional area makes it work effectively, on time, and on budget. In defining the goals, you must understand the importance of the goal, how it fits into the overall plan, the resources needed by function, and the consequence of not delivering that goal to the team in a quality fashion and on time.

Before you leave, it is useful to have each executive present/recap his/her functional goals that support the overall company plan and to begin to define the resources needed to get the job done as defined and in the time frame required. If you end the meeting on a high note of enthusiasm and everyone looks a little challenged, then you have done your job. Your team is thinking and worrying about getting the job done, which is a good thing. The plan should be a challenge, but it should also be reasonably achievable to avoid any discouragement.

Once the thousand-day plan goals are set, you have the tools to help you guide your team members as a team and a reason for them to work productively with each other in an integrated manner. Your next step is to require each executive to fine-tune his/her specific functional objectives and the resources needed to achieve them.   They will do this task working with their own team, creating a common interest and perhaps a bond at each functional level. When all this is done, you have the basis for the financial budget for the first year of the thousand-day plan. A little more fine-tuning with strong support from your chief financial officer, and you are ready to take this to the next level. This will take place over a period of weeks, at which time it would be wise to have a second executive planning session to go over a final review of all the goals and objectives in total and by function, in preparation for the board presentation.

You will set the final schedule with the board and it is best to have your executives participate in the presentation.   Don't spend months doing this; four to six weeks is enough time from start to finish. The important issue is that the team and the board now have a thousand-day plan to guide them. Yes, the plan will change, but the general direction is set for the first version of the plan, and it is your job to make sure this plan is updated and refined. This is your tool to help you manage the company, so use it wisely. It is also your tool to keep your executive team working as one unit for a common cause, so again, use it wisely for this purpose also.

Over the years I have observed the activities of a number of dysfunctional management teams, and in just about every case, the root cause of the dysfunction was the leader. When executives in a team do not work together as a team, the politics begin, and some members turn on others or on everyone else. This cancer must be eliminated from any organization, and you as the CEO are charged with fixing this problem. Use the goals that come from a thousand-day plan to help unite your team behind a common purpose, and you will be glad you did. If you don't have such a plan, a set of goals and objectives, and you have a team that has trouble working with each other and getting along, it is time to look in the mirror. Alternatively, if you have a bad apple, get rid of it and replace it with a good team member. Again, this is your job, and this is why you get the big bucks to be CEO. Make it happen!

Team Configuration
Proactively define and balance your management team structure based on the strategic and tactical needs of the company first. If your company has a significant challenge in the drug-development area or the clinical area or the sales and marketing area, make sure to recruit the best people you can find for the job. You can never get someone too good, and it is always best to hire the smartest and best people you can find, even when they are smarter than you. Weak CEOs typically hire weak management while strong CEOs typically hire strong management. Whether you realize it or not, you as the CEO are often judged by the quality of your management team. If it is weak, then you look weak. If you are worried about a new hire taking your job, then you have a problem. Otherwise, find the best people you can find and compensate them to join and stay with you for the long term.

A good executive will define and work a great plan, do it efficiently, intelligently, and cost effectively, and achieve the desired results. This is what you want. Your job as the CEO is not to do your team members' jobs but to make sure they are doing their jobs. More importantly your job is to create synergy in a team to enable it to achieve more than it could as the sum of its parts. When an executive needs help, then provide that executive with support from all areas as needed. When he/she is on a roll, let him/her run. When an executive reaches a point when he/she can no longer keep up with the rest of the team and is falling down on objectives, it is your job as the CEO to make a change in that important position. You are making this change out of respect for the other hard working executives on your team, and because it is the right decision to make for the shareholders. That person may be a good friend, a loyal employee, even a relative; it does not matter. You need to make the change, and the sooner the better. This is what you as the CEO get paid to do, and you need to make this difficult decision and implement it.

Take Away Items

- Prepare a 1,000-day plan early in the cycle and recruit your team for the long term.
- Communicate your strategic plan and mission, and continuously modify it as needed.
- Hire the very best people that you can get to work for you at all times. Work hard at keeping those people.
- Create a culture within the organization, through your executive team, that embraces the company's objectives and speaks to them often.

CHAPTER 8

MANAGING OPERATIONAL EFFECTIVENESS

Management is cause; all else is effect.
—JIM BURKE, FORMER CHAIRMAN, JOHNSON & JOHNSON

I once worked for a company whose chairman offered the above quote about management. To this day I think this quote says it all regarding the importance of good management. My years of business experience have only confirmed that these are truly words of wisdom.

In this chapter you will be exposed to thoughts and experiences that may help to contribute to strong team effectiveness and efficiency.

What makes the management functions within of a life science company unique and even more challenging is the very expensive, long product gestation cycles. In the most extreme situation a newly synthesized molecule could take ten years to progress from discovery to product launch and the total investment for such a drug could be $500 million dollars or more. Such a scenario involves a simple math average cost over the ten-year period of $137,000 per calendar day. Normally, expenses are lower than average at the early stages, and much higher than average at the later clinical stage. However, I believe you can agree with my point that each day is expensive and development time matters. Let's also view this situation from a different prospective, as follows:

To emphasis this point I would offer the analysis below for your consideration.

Task	Manager A	Manager B	Difference
Animal Research Study	30 days	40 days	10 days
Dose Form Development	3 months	4 months	1 month
Phase II Clinical Trial	24 months	32 months	8 months

In the above example, two different managers conducted identical studies. Manager B took longer to complete each task than Manager A. We will presume that the quality of the work and the outcomes were identical for each manager.

Yes there were differences in the completion times of the three studies and in some situations the differences were small. However, in each situation, Manager B took 33% more time to complete the task and possibly 20-33% more in cost. As previously noted, a simple math average of $137,000, each day matters. A week lost can cost close to $1 million. However, the most compelling cost factor is not as obvious, and that is opportunity cost that may include:

- If it took 33% more time to obtain drug approval and therefore market launch, that would mean the competitive drug that is right behind yours in development is catching up to you and might beat you to the market.
- A delayed product launch could lead to a lower long-term market share position of your product and hundreds of millions of dollars in lost profit over the total number of marketing years of that product.
- The loss of only one protected market year of product revenues and profits could be substantial involving tens of millions of dollars.

What the above indicates is that efficiency and effectiveness matters, and it is management that causes that result. The uniquely longer product to market gestation cycles in your industry means more expensive hang time for a product in development. You and your management team must always focus on the need to get a quality development project completed as soon as possible to optimize the strategic market and profit opportunity of that product. It is too easy to loose this very important strategic issue over a period of years, but it is extremely important in terms of building overall company value. When it is exit time, the remaining market life and market share level of this product will have everything to do with the level of the exit payout.

Let's reflect a little about managing at the executive level and other levels.

When you were a first line supervisor you spent a fair amount of time training lower level employees and lining up their assignments for them. Most of the time you are assisting them with increasing their technical skills enabling them to do improve their job performance.

As a middle manager you learned to delegate more to your supervisors. Your supervisors were somewhat inexperienced at times so you still invested in training and providing directions as needed to help them become better supervisors.

As an executive you learn that you have to give your managers more autonomy and work with improving their management skills and their skill sets for higher positions of responsibility. You helped them develop planning skills and worked with them to hold their staffs accountable for quality and timeliness. You provide both direction and if necessary, directions, to help them be more effective. You encourage them to make presentations, recommendations, and give them exposure by bringing them with you occasionally to executive discussions.

As a CEO you are working with executives that come with proven management experience. They have their own styles that have worked for them and they come with plenty of their own management experiences and lessons. You always give executives direction, not directions. If you have to routinely give them directions you have the wrong person in the job.Yes, it is important to let each executive run his/her own shop they way they know best. Yes it is important that the activities of that executive are totally in line with the key business objectives and that he/she are managing their area of responsibility. As a CEO you tend to manage your direct executive reports behavior and priorities through things such as objectives, vs. actually managing the executive.

Management Effectiveness

Synergy is the ability to cause the whole to be great than the sum of the parts. You invest you energy making sure that your executive team is doing everything they can, in a quality way, to move product development toward a market launch without unnecessary delays or avoidable problems. It is critically important that you manage the key overall company development objectives continuously for best results. On occasion this may mean using your position to eliminate a road block, to add a resource to continue, to get another executive or two to help our with solving part of a problem. It does not mean that in your position you need to, or should, micromanage all development activities. Manage the company objectives through your responsible executives and make sure they are managing the people and processes necessary to make it all happen. Your ability to create synergy with your management team by enabling and encouraging them to work together as a one integrated unit will result in stand out performance and make for a happier team.

You configured and recruited an excellent management team based on your chosen business strategy. That team can operate like a herd of independent cats, or it can be an efficient machine to get you where you need to go. As the leader of the team it is now your time to lead, and lead you must, because the stakes and the risks are high in your industry.

A good team will either turn bad or break up without good leadership. You are the chief executive officer for a reason and your success as a leader depends on your ability to manage your team to bring out the best in each executive.

At the executive level there is often a great deal of ego and aggressive behavior. Perhaps this is simply because it is another group of high achievers that want to go higher. That attribute is attractive to you and is one of the main reasons you hired them. Your challenge is to take each of your executives to a higher level in the achievement of a higher goal by working as one team.

A common set of business objectives can often serve as the unifying agent to bring a team together. By leading the team to build a set of meaningful and achievable objectives it helps to form unity. Also, going forward as conflicts emerge, and they inevitable will, it provides you the opportunity to solve executive conflict by going back to the objectives and developing a conflict solution that is business objective focused, and not personal. To do this you start with the big picture plan but it is important that you create a process that enables the team to develop an operating plan that they can consider their own.

Please bear with me as I share some of my management thoughts
Delegation

I have found that it is useful to attempt to have a balanced team, with all members loaded with key responsibilities to keep them busy and out of trouble at all times. There are certain things that only a CEO can do. You must interact with your board of directors, your committee, your key shareholders and investment bankers. However, you should design your team so you can delegate everything that does not have to be done by the CEO, making sure all the objectives of the company are being achieved. Your primary job is to set the plan and make sure the entire team is working on your plan with regard to achievements, budget, and timing. Stay involved with progress, hold everyone accountable, but let your team execute the operations with your support as required. Insert yourself when needed to shore up a problem, fix and then move away and let's you executives finish the process.

Team Balance

I consider titles of senior VP (vice president), executive VP, and "regular" VP to be problematic. A title is an ego and a pecking-order issue. It is a way for one executive to say that he/she is more important than another. A CEO is often also the president, and then there are the CEO's direct reports that comprise the executive team. Reporting directly to the CEO is all that should really matters to a senior executive; so don't feed the ego problem with special titles that appear to be some kind of pecking order when it really is not. Deal with this situation in a way that does not cause problems by simply taking the approach that you wish to simplify your organizational structure for now, and in the future

Dysfunction destroys efficiency and effectiveness.

Company politics and/or disharmony simply must not be an active part of the executive team. Often the problem presents itself, whether latent or obvious; it usually never really goes away, with the rare exception of in the very best teams. Your executive team must work together in harmony, with or without you your immediate presence. In observing dysfunctional teams, I have noted that in most cases there was either a lack of cohesive objectives to keep everyone on the same page, or there were team members that just were no up to the task and were pulling the team down.

When you have executives that just simply cannot get along, you have two choices: either fix the problem or replace them. Sometimes sending them both on a trip for a common purpose allows them to get to know each other a little better. Often this can result in them obtaining a better understanding each other both personally and professionally and, at best, some level of bonding. Sometimes you just have to replace the bad apple (or two). In most cases with a little work on your part you eliminate much of the nonsense by focusing everyone's time and energy on a meaningful set of company goals and objectives.

It is inevitable that as you grow and the company's management challenges increase there will be executives that cannot keep up. To maximize the effectiveness and efficiency of a team with growing challenges, it is necessary to cull weak or struggling team members periodically. This is no different that changing players on a sports team. This is what head coaches do and it is a normal part of achieving excellence. If an executive is a problem the change is usually an easy one and you will cause their exit from the company. However, the overwhelming majority of these changes will probably involve replacing a great loyal person, perhaps someone that was with you from the beginning, with a much more seasoned and experience executive. You work for the shareholders, and achievement of the key goals and objectives are what you are being paid to do. You accomplish those difficult achievements with an outstanding team that must continuously improve itself to be able to perform at higher levels. This will be a very difficult decision for you to make and it will give you great stress. You must replace that executive, that friend, that relative, that neighbor, because that is what the person in the CEO's position must do. You owe this to your team and your shareholders. Perhaps that person can be put in a meaningful position that specializes in an area that they are very good at and can make great contributions but on a more narrow scale. Perhaps that person is having family problems or health problems and they need fewer responsibilities. Be fair and reasonable with this employee but make sure he/she is replaced at the executive level of the company with a more seasoned, experienced executive that is capable of performing at the higher levels your future demands. If you cannot do this then your board needs to be thinking about replacing you because this is your job. No one said being a CEO was easy. There is plenty of good that goes with the job and there is the very difficult side to causing a business to succeed. A lesson from this is to be very careful and thoughtful about granting fancy titles to your start-up team. One or more of those VP's may be the person described above. It is better to use titles like manager, or director than

VP in the beginning and by doing this and also by communicating the need for an executive that can continuously handle higher levels of performance, it suggests that a group of VP's will be joining the company at some time. If you have not learned this already, you will after you have to terminate, demote, or reassign people that you have worked with for a long time and have been loyal to you. Avoid overcommitting titles and it will help to make these changes easier when they need to be made.

Working together on projects towards a common outcome

Usually key business objectives require the coordinated support of several executives to achieve success so it forces them to work together for a common outcome. For example, if you want a successful product launch, you have to have the right quantity of finished goods inventory, a ready pipeline of raw materials, and the right mix of each product SKU's (stock keeping units) to support the launch plan. Your VP of operations is responsible for this key task. The sales and marketing executive is responsibility for developing a sales plan by product in units, by month, for a period of at least six months in advance. This enables the manufacturing executive to build the desired amount of finished-goods launch inventory and stage raw materials for forecasted sales for the first six months.

The launch plan is expensive and consumes cash in the way of working capital for inventory and receivables. Launches result in either too much inventory, too little or too much of one SKU, or too little of another SKU. The executive team has to have a clear plan with flexibility built in to best manage inventory levels during the launch period because there is always a great deal of uncertainly in a launch. General Eisenhower developed a massive plan for D Day but did he really know what the outcome would be? Your VP of finance will need to know the cash needs of the launch and the revenue and cost projections related to that launch. The company needs good planning to be able to determine the cost of the launch, properly prepare for it, and know whether the actual sales are at, above, or below the plan. You can let the three VPs work this out for your periodic review, but this would be an example of how a proactive planning approach by the CEO months in advance will eliminate this potential area of conflict. You simply state to your team that you require a detailed launch plan by month, in dollars and units, and you need it by a certain date, perhaps six months before the planned launch date. When all four of you meet you will then discuss the details and adjust the plan as a group. It is always a good idea to have the executives present their respective parts of the plan to the board. It gets them motivated to do an even better job, and your board will appreciate the extra operational information, if they have the time to listen to it.

Good leadership prevents conflict by having your team focus on the key business objectives. With a new team that has not worked together in the past, it is very important that you provide more leadership the first time you engage in such an exercise. Your team members will usually respect you for it, they will appreciate that it helped them to do their jobs properly, and the next time, they will know it is coming and what to do and plan for. Remember, your team members know how to do their jobs very well; you just need to coach them.

Work and communicate as a team as much as possible

Too often the CEO has the team in place but chooses to speak with each executive separately. This does not bode well for team building and creates a culture that may lead to distrust. Your team must know that you strongly believe that each team member always plays a role in key company objectives and they all contribute more or less to one objective or another. If you do this properly, they will consider it a privilege to participate in such meetings. Being able to be part of the key executive planning process is recognition of that executive's high-level status in the company. You will have plenty of occasions to speak with one or two executives privately, but the group meetings will always contribute to team building, and good team building often leads to long-term success. Again, all this is business, not personal. Even if you think some executive on your team may not directly contribute to the meeting, invite him/her anyway. You will be surprised how many times he/she will come up with a way to help the effort in some way that you did not consider.

Recognition

When the team performs well as team make sure you use this opportunity to congratulate all of them. Everyone enjoys a good pat on the back occasionally and if this helps to build teamwork it is a plus. It is also useful to recognize their achievement while they are also present in a board meeting.

Matrix Management

Another way to help a team to work more closely is to create program awareness and accountability. Let me use the following example within the development function.

Many projects, people, things, and challenges exist within a development function. In short, there are lots of moving parts that at all times need to produce high-quality work and integrate with other activities in a timely fashion.

Any development function has a complex array of people, equipment, facilities, and projects, all of which need to be planned, budgeted, and accounted for. The senior executive in charge of this function must have the knowledge and management skills to effectively and efficiently drive this function. In addition, it is very important to develop a great team of department heads that can drive their respective functions and build their teams to perform at their best. Again, management at all levels "is cause; all else is effect." Most of your company budget will be spent on development, so never cut corners on the quality of your management. Good management will drive progress; make the hard decisions needed to keep or terminate a project or a manager, and keep spending in line to enable you to achieve your goals and objectives within budget. I cannot emphasize how important it is to have excellent managers in charge of your highest-spending operating function.

A matrix management system can work well in an organization with multiple projects and programs at varying stages of development. A matrix system involves a network of contributing parties that form a management matrix by project with one or more project managers, depending on the size and complexity of the development activities.

Matrix Management

Department functions	Manager project A	Manager project B	Manager project C
Intellectual property	X	X	X
Chemistry	X	X	X
Drug formulation	X	X	X
Drug metabolism	X	X	X
Toxicology	X	X	X
GMC Mfg. of clinical supplies	X	X	X
IND preparation	X	X	
Phase I clinical study	X		

In this case the department heads focus on performance of the functional development activities, and the project managers schedule, budget, project, and report on overall project status. It can be useful to include intellectual property in this mix in an effort to make sure it retains executive visibility and receives the proper support to achieve the strategic goals of the company. A matrix management system involves two groups working on the same activity with a different, but supportive, objective. If the size of your organization and the number of programs can be justified, a matrix management approach to development programs can be very useful to the entire executive team. More eyes on critical programs from a different prospective are always useful.

This same matrix approach can be applied to a product launch, a regulatory package completion effort or any other key task that involves multiple disciplines and disciplined timelines. It builds teamwork and accountability at all management levels. In addition, such a process tends to highlight problems and challenges to the executives levels faster so management put solutions in place those issue sooner than later. As your programs progress towards the partnering stage, the matrix system approach will enable you to present programs to partners in a meaningful, professional manner.

The thousand-day plan goals and objectives. The first step involved in enabling your executives to fuse as one unit is to state the existing key strategic goals and objectives you set for the company. Next is to take the time to plan the desired executive team structure needed to get to the end of your thousand-day plan. This should be a different management configuration than exists today, and it will involve dividing more executive responsibilities, perhaps adding some additional direct reports to you. By projecting this you are essentially building some specialization into your team to achieve key objectives that require higher knowledge and/or experience on the part of the executive position. You need to be objective in doing this and think in terms of the executive positions needed to deliver results that support company goals, not individual personalities. The CEO needs to decide on the structure and responsibilities of the executive team. It is acceptable to share this with your those executives that report directly to you as they all need to look at the big picture and accept the fact that you are organizing and developing a team to take the company successfully into the future. Executive level meetings like this are for mature, serious executives because it is addressing the leadership solution to the key strategic goals and objectives of the company. If certain executives have trouble rising to the occasion then it might present the first clue as to whether they should be part of the long terms executive team or not. None of this is personal; it is all business, and very serious business. Remember, *Management is cause; all else is effect.*

Take Away Issues

- Remember that a team is like a chain, and a chain is only as strong as it weakest link
- A CEO by definition must constantly multitask and deal with the problems and challenges involving multiple functions simultaneously.
- You are always the head coach of your team's operating strategy

- Your long term success has everything to do with how you manage your team and your company objectives
- If you are not creating team synergy, you are not managing

CHAPTER 9

COMPENSATION

Cheap labor is not cheap.

I n chapter 4 we discussed issues involving a compensation committee. In this chapter we will discuss the concepts, objectives, and execution of a good compensation program for all employees. Your objective should always be to recruit the best employees, consultants, and advisors you can find and keep them. It is often easier to find them than to keep them so you want to avoid unnecessary turnover especially when it involves key members of your team, Board, or other 3rd party support teams. Remember, you cannot do this alone and it can only be done with a team and managing that team is your responsibility and your challenge as the CEO.

First it is important to separate those being compensated into several groups, as follows:

- Board directors / board committee members
- Executive management team
- Nonexecutive management
- Non management employees

Board / Board Committee Level
Let's begin at the board level and distinguish between board members that are part of the executive management team and independent,

outside, third party board members. Board compensation is normally provided to third-party board members to attract them to your team, and company executives are typically not paid any additional compensation for their board participation.

Outside board members can bring much value to a company. Board members can provide credibility, contacts, technical wisdom, business wisdom, practical experience, financing sources, industry sources, partnering sources, and so on. Board members are compensated for their time on board and board committee matters. To the extent the company wishes to have certain board members assist in occasional, periodic consulting roles, such activities would involve a separate consulting agreement. Any such agreement with a board member requires board approval.

A large, profitable company has the benefit of attracting high-quality board members with an annual cash compensation package for board and committee participation. Additional compensation is provided in the form of a stock option package or company shares. The amount of the package is something that varies considerably from company to company. In very large billion-dollar companies, it is not unusual for a board member to receive cash compensation in excess of $100K per year plus equity. In such large companies, there are much higher demands for board-member time, and to some extent it becomes a "job."

In smaller, not-yet-profitable development companies with cash challenges, it is not possible to provide high levels of cash compensation. In such situations the company will compensate for travel and other direct expenses and provide a meeting-based cash board fee and an extra cash fee for committee participation. Board members are issued stock option contracts and/or stock grants, and the level of these programs has everything to do with the quality of company, the management team, and the board members' interest in associating with the company. It is always wise to allocate at least 1–3 percent of your equity to board/committee-related compensation matters.

Executive Management Team

Investors want the executives to have an incentive to make the company successful and stay with and solve future problems when they surface. The concept of "golden handcuffs" has merit in these situations. To be able to attract and retain high-quality talent, the executive compensation program should involve the following:

- Cash compensation:
    - Competitive annual salaries consistent with industry standards and job responsibilities
    - Annual cash bonuses
- Equity incentives: This program normally involves the granting of a stock option contract or another form of equity incentive. Stock option grants are the most common; these contracts provide the executive the right to purchase a defined number of shares, at a defined price, for a defined period. Usually such contracts vest, or are earned, over time. Vesting periods normally run three to five years until all the options in the package are vested. Such agreements may also involve registration rights, acceleration clauses for a change in control, and other features that may increase or decrease the value of these contracts. Aside from cash compensation, the equity incentive package is key to most executives.
- Employee benefits: Today's executives expect the following benefit plans:
    - Insurance
        - Medical insurance, supplemented by the company to a certain extent
        - Disability insurance (short term)
        - Life insurance (group) availability
    - Retirement plan availability
        - 401(k)/SEP
        - Some level of company matching contribution in cash or company shares

- Defined vacation plan
- Other benefits that may be appropriate for a certain company and/or executive

Clearly the CEO should have the best compensation package and the greatest equity incentive to make the company successful. It is also normal for the CEO to have the same employee benefits package as all employees, with exceptions for any recruitment-related concessions. The executive team has the highest levels of annual cash salary, cash bonuses, and equity incentives. There are no rigid standards for such programs, and it is important to understand that it is the executive team members that lead their respective teams to achieve operating goals. Because the executive team directly influences the behavior and activities of the rest of the employee team, these disproportionate compensation levels are warranted and acceptable.

Non Executive Management

The same compensation concepts apply to this management group. These managers should have an incentive/compensation level higher than that of non-management employees, but lower than that of the executive team. This nonexecutive management team usually involves several management levels from middle management to first-level managers, and compensation should be administered appropriately. Many companies begin to provide equity incentive compensation at the first-line management level of the organization. This is also an incentive for employees to want to achieve a management position and take more responsibility in the company, especially as they will now begin to direct the daily activities of a larger group of employees.

Non Management Employees

With the exception of the equity incentives, all the above applies to non-management employees. Equity incentives are not normally offered to all non-management employees; however, there are exceptions, especially in small start-up companies, where employment risk tends to be higher. Personally I have always favored the idea of granting equity incentives to all permanent full-time employees, even if very small, because it creates an incentive at all levels to perform to achieve the stated company objectives.

Overall Considerations

It is important to be crystal clear about compensation programs and policies with all employees. It is useful to prepare company policies on such matters even if they are short and cover just the most important issues about a program. Misunderstandings often occur when you fail to do so.

It is also important to conduct annual salary reviews, provide annual bonus systems, and treat all your employees with the respect that they deserve.

Finally, it is important to cull low-performing team members as required, out of respect for the team members that make substantial contributions to the company. Just tolerating low-performing people on the team, even if your company can afford to do so, is not a good business practice. Sometimes it is best for certain employees to leave the company and find a position more suitable for their desires and talents. You should always strive to improve the overall quality of your entire employee team by recruiting the best, training the existing, and replacing low-performing employees with new outstanding recruits.

Take Away Issues

- Greed is a terrible thing and it interferes with final outcomes in a very negative way. Respect your team for both their strategic and tactical contributions all of which enrich you personally in time. You cannot do this job alone so share the wealth and provide fair and balanced equity incentives to those that can really make a difference.

- It is difficult to recruit the very best talent and it is even more difficult to keep the very best talent. The good ones go first so make sure they don't have a reason to look elsewhere. If you don't take care of your best and brightest someone else will and that someone else will be thanking you for training them.
- Happy employees are productive employees. Create work conditions and employee compensation packages that are fair and competitive to keep productivity high and turnover low.

CHAPTER 10

THE COMMERCIALIZATION PHASE

Partnering or Product Sales Business Models

It ain't over till it's over.
—*YOGI BERRA*

Partnering/Licensing Pathway

General

You have chosen to develop your products and technology to a point that enables you to partner them, with the partner assuming all future development costs. There are a number of important steps/phases required to close all partnering agreement, as follows:

General Preparation for the Partnering Process

Someone once said that selling is 90 percent preparation, 10 percent delivery. You will appreciate how true this statement is after you complete this section. If you think partnering and the business-development function in general is not selling, you are mistaken. Trust and confidence drive a relationship. Keep in mind you will be dealing with smart people like your self, and oftentimes they are more experienced and have done many deals in the past. They have seen all the games and have little tolerance for them. They value trust in you, the data, and your company culture.

In participating in many of these activities, I have always found it useful to prepare the following materials:

Introduction/Overview Materials (Non confidential)

Business development is a process with many steps/phases. The first step is to verify that your target actually has a strategic interest in a product or territory like yours. If not, you don't want to share information with them and waste your time and theirs. I have found it useful to develop two sets of materials for this purpose, as follows:

- The one-page teaser: The first one is a one-page non-confidential "teaser" that generally describes your product or technology program at a high level This document should include possible future indications and markets of interest and is e-mailed to an interested party.
- Non-confidential product or technology overview: This is usually a short (ten to twelve slides) presentation e-mailed to an interested party.

Note: You may find it useful to send the teaser first if you are not sure or know little about the prospect. If there is interest, then it makes sense to send the slide presentation. If you begin with the teaser, the next step would normally be the slide overview.

Nondisclosure Agreement (NDA)

By now you have sent introduction materials to and spoken with at least one representative of the target, which has reviewed the opportunity internally and would like to learn more. Up until this point, you have shared only non-confidential information with those parties. It is useful to retain the services of a corporate attorney, and it is best if that person is also a securities attorney. We all have NDAs, but it is best that you develop one that is acceptable to your company and use it. I would caution you, however, that most Big Pharma companies have their own NDA forms, and you may have to acquiesce on a few agreement terms to proceed. This agreement is useful in the event someone steals something from you and you are able to prove it. (Good luck on the latter point.) Now keep in mind that signing an NDA does not give a target a right to every secret you have. However, it does require that the target keep confidential the select group of material, thoughts, ideas, and so on that you share with it.

Target Prospect List

Develop a list of prospective targets for your products and technologies. Now is the time to formalize this list and populate the list with names, titles, phone numbers, and e-mail addresses if you can. More on this later, but for now your preparation includes this important list, which you will put to use as soon as you are ready to launch your business-development effort.

Developing a Detailed Electronic Data Library

Partnering/licensing is about preparing a convincing data package on a promising product candidate or technology platform. What you have is of interest to your targets, and that is why they are talking with you. However, never forget that they need to find out whether you have something they might wish to invest in, and they also worry about how you could hurt them if there were material undisclosed issues and events. The best measure of your credibility and integrity is the data package you develop for their review. This data package, or data library, will be the basis for all the due diligence efforts your targets conduct, and you will be judged by its form, content, completeness, and accuracy. Please, no games, no shallow speculations—just the facts.

Rule 1: Make it easy, make it complete, anticipate their questions, and provide thoughtful, accurate answers or comments that address potential questions. This data library will be reviewed by a number of professionals within your prospective partner's organization. Many of them you may never meet, but they will be forming impressions all along the way based on your data package. Their job is to be stone cold objective and find good long-term opportunities for the company while avoiding painful problematic investments.

Rule 2: You may have trade secrets and/or highly sensitive information that you choose not to disclose until a later time in the discussions. You have the right to hold back until a later time, but it is best to describe those restrictions so that everything is on the table. Know that if your discussions continue to go on, you will then be disclosing this more sensitive information. Thus, this information also should be properly organized and disclosed like everything else in your electronic library.

Rule 3: The easy packages, meaning the more organized and complete solicitation packages, get processed first and fastest. It is best to use an electronic data library and digitize everything. This way documents can easily be passed on to various functional experts within the target, which they will appreciate. Doing this right takes a fair amount of effort but, if done correctly, will be useful and applicable to all targets for a particular product/platform. This effort involves large files, and you can use Dropbox or some other similar tool to transfer this data.

You may wish to organize your electronic data library as follows:

1. Table of Contents: List every section of the library.
2. Intellectual Property: Table of contents. Provide digital files of all patent filings and patent grants by country, by invention. It is useful to begin this section with summary of your patent estate and further display it by invention and prosecution status, and by geography. Provide every communication with the patent office and any summaries of verbal interactions you may have. Update this as needed to keep it current. Again, make this one very easy to follow and understand for both patent attorneys and management.

3. Preclinical Package: Table of contents. Provide all animal study protocols; reports and summaries performed. Leave none out, especially those that may be unfavorable. Include toxicology, ADME (absorption, distribution, metabolism, excretion studies, dosing titration and efficacy by kg, stability, dose form development, etc.

4. IND Submission: Table of contents. This is the originally submitted package, even if it was updated later. Provide any updates separately. Communications with the agency regarding this IND submission need to be included, and it is best to put them in chronological order.

5. GMP Clinical Supplies / Chemistry and Manufacturing: Table of contents. Provide all detailed information related specifically to the production batch of clinical supplies and the GMP validation effort associated with that batch. Unless it is proprietary, you should provide active ingredient synthesis/production information.

6. Phase I Clinical Study Program: Table of contents. Begin with a summary report. Provide protocols, all agency interactions, study site training/audits, copies of original patient records, statistical summaries, and reports, all adverse events, details on any dropouts, and all other matters that are relevant to understand how this study (these studies) was conducted and the good and bad results experienced.

7. Phase II Clinical Study Program: Table of contents. Begin with a summary report on safety and efficacy observed. By study, provide protocols, all agency interactions, study site reports, all adverse events, and details of any patient dropouts, and report any finding of interest regarding any segments of the population with noteworthy efficacy or safety issues.

8. Phase III: Considerations: You probably will not be conducting the phase III programs yourself if you plan to partner. However, this may present an opportunity for you to provide some pearls of wisdom based on your review and experience with the phase I and II programs. Again, keep in mind a number of people will review these documents, all forming opinions throughout their

review. You might wish to see this section as an opportunity to sell the reason why you think an expensive phase III program will be successful and justified.

Confidential Slide Presentation

If the discussions are moving forth in a positive way, then at some point you will make a technical presentation to the target's licensing team. This presentation may take place at your location or the target's. For me it was always best to present at the target's location because I then had the opportunity to meet more of their people than if they had formed a smaller team to fly to my location.

A slide presentation, properly organized and presented, gives you the opportunity to present your technology and management team, and it gives the target the opportunity to ask their initial set of questions as a group in a somewhat organized fashion. You can use the slide presentation vehicle to break the ice and have each side better understand and appreciate all parties more quickly than if you held a series of meetings on one subject at a time. This meeting of introduction is the time to ask the big, broad questions that need answers. If there is still interest after this meeting, the formal due diligence process will begin. My preference is to have this technical presentation prior to opening up the data library to the partner, but these events could occur simultaneously depending on the partner and the level of interest. You may find that targets insist on reviewing the data library prior to the meeting so they can be better prepared. I have done it both ways, and it is a judgment call that has everything to do with how serious you think the target is.

Prospecting

You must be creative in your prospecting efforts. Yes, of course you will solicit the current-day leaders, but there are other parties to consider that may be hungry to increase their market positions. You could license this to Big Pharma, or you could partner, merge, or joint-venture this to a smaller company able to convince you that it has the funding and talent in place to pull it off. You may also wish to consider possible targets from other, new sales channels that are trying to find exclusive products to distribute and disrupt the current marketplace. Be open-minded about whom you choose to solicit, but at the same time, avoid soliciting everyone in the phone book. If you have more than twenty prospects, you might want to do some screening to trim it down to a more manageable list.

Once you develop your prime prospect (target) list, begin to learn a little more about the management structure of that organization. The important issue is to find the right individual to introduce your package to. In a large company, this is most likely a business-development executive who has the principal responsibility for reviewing promising new opportunities that fit his/her company's strategic development plan. In a smaller company, your contact might be the CEO. If the target involves something a little off beat, such as a new sales channel, you will have to do a little homework to find the person that might handle such matters. It could be the CEO, or a marketing or sales executive, or someone else with a high level of interest.

Now you have a name. It is always highly recommended to place a phone call and speak with that point person before you send in your package. Such a call is always useful and will prevent your package from getting lost in a pile of other packages. A successful partnering effort often has one or two internal champions for the project that are selling it internally for you, even if you don't realize it. As the business-development point person, you must nurture that relationship to your advantage, feeding it with quality information and service. The last comment to make in this section is that you as the point person must fully understand that the negotiations for this technology begin with the first phone call and continue throughout the entire process, involving all people, all data, and all communications at all times with everyone involved. You need to advise your team members that everything they say and do can and will be held against them. So enjoy yourself, build friendships, but never let your guard down. You are always in a negotiation forum.

Due Diligence Process

This is where it counts. Most likely you will be interacting with a larger organization whose work force is highly specialized with many experts in many areas. They already presume you are not going to tell them all the bad news and that you might amplify the good news. You have to prove them wrong and build their trust and confidence, and you can only do that one way—with data. The target's team members are busy doing their regular jobs in the company and are on temporary assignment to complete the due diligence on your technology as it pertains to their specific areas of expertise. They were selected to be part of this due diligence team because they are experienced, smart, and skilled in their arts, and they can be counted on to be objective. While they wish to be friendly and cordial, they are not here to make friends; instead they are here to get an important job done for their company. You have the same objectives. Nevertheless, enjoy yourselves because this can be a lot of fun in between all the hard work.

I cannot overemphasize the importance of doing a first-class job on developing your electronic data library. Often companies will rush this effort to get started faster because they need cash. While that is certainly understandable, it could turn into a mistake. Like everything in life, you get one chance to make a first impression. You and others will be making first impressions to a number of people over a period of months. However, the data library will have lasting impression, and it will represent the quality and professionalism of your team. A good package will go a long way in establishing confidence, trust, and credibility; a poorly developed package could terminate the discussions early.

Usually the process begins with a technical meeting involving several disciplines. Eventually, the counterpart disciplines pair off and begin a series of separate conversations about their respective areas. This will occur in all areas, and at some point there will be a summary of issues. There are always issues, so expect them, but the fewer the better. One good thing about an issues list is that it shows what, at least for now, is not on the list. So you work with the issues and explain and convince until solutions can be provided. In the world of sales, these issues are called objections, and as soon as you can remove all the objections, you are ready to begin talking about a deal. Not all issues are deal breakers, but some could be, and if so, you might be hearing this often from other parties. If there is something you can do about it, just do it so you eliminate the objection.

Now during this process the business-development person needs to be on top of all issues and should be communicating all this to the executive team. Most everybody in the line functions will be involved to some extent, and they all need to know the importance of presenting a full information picture at all times. You need to do this with engagements with all prospective partners. This is your future revenue stream, and everything depends on it, so it will require the full support of the company.

Negotiations

Rule 1: Never discuss business terms with your prospective partners until there is a buying signal from the partner. It is completely inappropriate to discuss specific terms up front or suggest terms before the time is right. It is OK to discuss, when asked, overall general deal concepts such as "front payments and royalties on sales," but avoid taking the bait at all times. A buying signal occurs only after the due diligence process has been completed and the objections list has been deemed acceptable. This will occur months later.

Rule 2: Never have more than one person lead the negotiation effort. This is the time for one and only one point person, only one captain on the ship, and one person speaking at a time. Your failure to adhere to this process will inevitably result in a costly misstep.

Rule 3: As previously mentioned, anything you say or do can and will be held against you. Do your job, be sociable, but keep your guard up at all times. The worst transfers of information occur over a drink, over a meal, in the car, or in e-mail. When you are in negotiations, it is like being on the one-yard line in football. Keep your head down, stay focused, and run the play that has been called.

Rule 4: Always retain the services of a good corporate attorney to help you with negotiations and contract development. It is best to discuss deal concepts with your attorney prior to your first negotiating session, not after several sessions, when it may be too late to modify terms. Keep in mind that the contract represents the entire agreement, and anything said or agreed to outside of the contract is not part of the deal. Always retain a professional to help with something this important. A great conceptual provision in the contract can be mutilated by clever legal language that effectively neutralizes any benefit. In all contracts, words matter, and only the words that are in the contract.

Closing the Deal

The infamous Yogi Berra once said, "It ain't over till it's over." Until your contract is signed by both sides and is counter approved by all boards of directors, and shareholders if necessary, and until the money clears, your deal is not over. One experience I will share with you involved an $18 million acquisition deal that took six months of daily interaction to complete. The deal was fully negotiated; just waiting for a formality approval by the board of directors of a large multinational company because of the deal exceeded $5 million. Four days before the scheduled board meeting, we were informed that the lead board director for this project, which happened to be a new employee with the company, had simply changed his mind. My counterparts on the other side of this transaction were as surprised, shocked, and upset as we were, but that was the end of that deal. Six months of very hard work on the part of a number of people went up in smoke.

If either party in the transaction is a publicly traded company, a public announcement is probably needed. What will legally drive this public disclosure decision is whether one or both of the publicly traded companies consider this transaction a material disclosure. First it is necessary to keep all this confidential to avoid any insider trading violations, and second it is important for the parties to mutually agree on the language of the public announcement. The public announcement should immediately follow the execution of the agreement with board approval, and the agreement may indicate that the deal is subject to shareholder approval.

Consider the negotiations of all deals to be a business structure with a checklist of objections. As in selling, the parties need to remove all objections before a sale can take place. The same is true with negotiating a deal with a corporate partner. Contract negotiations from the time the parties agree, "Let's make a deal," to the consummation of that deal will take at minimum weeks and more likely months.

Heads of Agreement vs. Letters of Intent

I have never been a fan of letters of intent (LOIs) simply because they are typically nonbinding and often the language is too general creating ambiguity that creates problems later at the contract-development stage. The other issue with a letter of intent is that it often takes the pressure off closing a deal unless there is a deadline for closing. I prefer both sides to have the ability to walk away as this contributes to a healthy and timely negotiation process since either party can then do a deal with another party. However, an LOI can be useful in a fund raising exercise to show partnering intent, and often that is the reason for its use.

My preference is instead to work in good faith with a heads of agreement list. Technically the heads of agreement may not look all that different from a letter of intent, but it has always allowed me a little more flexibility in forcing the parties to work toward a tighter understanding of the agreement and get to a first draft contract a lot sooner. This is just my personal preference, and your experience might lead you to a different conclusion. In the end, nonbinding LOIs do not matter, and the only thing that does matter is a consummated definitive agreement. For me, that is where the negotiating parties need to focus their attention.

The first draft of the definitive agreement usually provides a good indication as to whether you are still negotiating the basic terms of the deal. Ideally, the parties agree to terms and discuss them in detail with regard to the letter and spirit of the terms with the involvement of their attorneys. Once the terms are agreed upon, the attorneys work together to draft the contract language to fit the terms negotiated and the spirit in which they were negotiated. My experience has been that if the first draft is way off, you may not have a deal at all, or best case, the deal is going to take a long time to conclude. If the first draft reflects the terms discussed, you can begin to be more confident that you may have a deal. Obtaining good value in a contract is not always just the terms or the conditions; often it is the language used to describe them, and here is where that good corporate attorney will provide you the service you need for this important achievement.

Product/Service Sales Pathway

General
You are a company that has now achieved revenue stage status to drive the growth of your business. Your plan is to market and sell your own products, and manufacture your products or have them manufactured by a third party. You are now considered to be a fully integrated operating company that can and will operate on its own without the continuous need to raise capital to survive. Now you actually have product revenues and the organization of your fully integrated operating company will be quite different from a development company.

For the purpose of this section, I presume that the sales company does not have an R&D function but is a product sales company with the strategy of introducing short life-cycle product-line extensions to build market share and profitability. To be successful you need to plan for and execute the following.

As a fully integrated operating company your business objective now relate to revenue growth, market share penetration, costs, margins and operating profit. You will also need to build into your plan new product introductions and line extensions of existing products. Lines extensions might involve different sizes or package of a similar product or an improved version of an existing product. A line extension differs from a new product in that it is based on an existing product and does not necessarily target a new market or new use. Line extensions are often introduced to capture higher market penetration, defend against a new competitive introduction, or simply take more retail shelf space to squeeze out competition.

Strategic Goals and Objectives

You will need to take the time with your team to define your business strategy for this company just like you would do for any other company. Be crystal clear about your long-term strategy and be prepared to communicate it often internally and externally. Your plan is to be prepared with the support and commitment of your entire executive who will then take the plan forward as their own with respect to their individual functional responsibilities.

Marketing Plan

Unlike drug development, market is warfare. Your job is either to expand the market with your product or take share from one or more of your competitors. Your experienced marketing executive will develop your marketing plan with this in mind knowing that the competition is not just going to lie down and let you take their business away from them. The marketing plan will begin with the key objectives agreed to in the strategic business plan as well as the tactical operating objectives that apply to year one of the strategic plan. Likewise the marketing plan you develop will address the strategic goal but will focus on the tactical objectives of the first year of the strategic business plan. It is useful for the marketing plan to identify the critical success factors that are expected to drive success. Your ability to focus on these key critical success factors will have much to do with your success.

Market Opportunity

It is always important to understand your target market and also the pros and cons of all the other competitive product entries within it. You should also know the strengths and weakness of the companies you are competing. Develop tactics and strategies that exploit the weaknesses of your competitor's products and your competitors against your strengths to gain market share and keep that market share from going back to your competition. For example, if one of your competitors has announced a product quality problem or if one of your competitors is going through a merger or acquisition this may present an opportunity of weakness that your sales force can and should exploit. Remember marketing is war, and war is hell!

Competitive Response

Your competitors know you are launching your product and have done as much research as they are able to on your new product, your sales team and your sales plan to the extend they can obtain that information. Once you actually launch into the marketplace they will increase that level of information through various sources. They will use this information to further develop and fine tune their tactical and strategic plans to counteract your product introduction in an effort to minimize their loss of market share by finding weaknesses in your product and plan. Depending on your product, prior to your official launch they may introduce very special inventory stocking deals to overload customers and sales channels with their product. By filling the pipeline in this manner it will make it difficult for you to succeed in obtaining big orders for your product introduction, but this is only a tactic. As they become more informed they will develop programs to both defend against your attack and develop counter attack programs to take back the market share your initially took from them. Look for and pay close attention to the reaction your competitors will have to your market launch.

Product Positioning

Every product has some advantages and some disadvantages, even yours. Do objective 3rd party market research to determine the true strengths and weaknesses of your product as determined by independent customers that represent your core target market. Do the same research on your competition starting with the top three competitors. Analyze these important results very objectively. If you cannot do that then get a 3rd party market research firm to objectively do the analysis for you, but get the true facts and a proper analysis.

Offense. Once you obtain the competitive analysis you should know the perceived strengths of your product vs. the perceived weaknesses of the top three competitive products Develop your plan to first capture the low hanging fruit, that is, the sales opportunities that are uniquely easy for your sale team to capture very quickly. Identify the next phase of the marketing and sales program that positions your product favorably against one or more of the competing products. Your advantage may be functionality, safety, price, durability, reliability etc. Sell your product strengths against products that have known or perceived weakness in the same area. For example, if competitive product A has two functions and does not work well in cold weather then sell that fact that your product works extremely well in cold weather and three functions including a new one that precludes the need for another piece of equipment, if that is your sales program. Develop the targeted message that a customer will relate to rather than just sell on price or as the new product on the market. You get the order if your product is better and the price is right, not just if the price is better. The sales objective is to present an offer that eliminates every buying objection you may have and provides the buyer the reason to order your product vs. the product that have been ordering for the past three years.

Defense. Occasionally, you might find a situation where your product is at a disadvantage to the competition. These are clearly more difficult situations and require creative solutions. For example, if your product has a real or perceived durability problem then you might consider a longer full replacement warranty along with an overnight replacement service, if that is financial feasible. More important is that you fix the durability problem ASAP and not have to deal with this sales objection. Just keep in mind that your competitors will continue to mention your problems with durability even after you fix the problem. That is just the way it is in the real world and you overcome this in time with positive information. When product quality issues surface it is important to involve the manufacturing executive quickly and if possible have him/her work with the sales/marketing executive in learning more about the problems directly from the field personnel that are experiencing the problem Get to know your critical problems quickly and first hand so you can implement real solid solutions as quickly as possible before they become major problems that interrupt the product launch. Product problems only give the competition a fantastic opportunity to beat you up in the field and take share back.

Targeting
Target your promotional efforts on those segments of the market that are best served by your new product entry. Just to use a war analogy, the infamous D Day landing involved a handful of beaches, not a complete frontal assault on the west coast of Europe. Establish a sales beach head first and then expand your program to widen its offering to a larger market segment. For example, if your product's best outstanding benefit is its ability to perform very well in cold weather and that is a desirable feature to your customers, then go there first and capture all the sales you can. While you are doing that then begin a beachhead with those customers that wish to have more functionality to reduce the amount of equipment they need to operate with. Start with the more acute customer need situations and then broaden as you gain acceptance. Know

your targets, their needs, and their fears.   Find them sell them, and bring home the orders.

Sales Plan

Your market research has directed you to certain segments of the market that represent a ripe opportunity for your product introduction. So develop marketing programs that initially go after the low-hanging fruit while focusing on the strategic shift in this market segment or segments that you believe will develop to your advantage. Develop your sales plan to know specifically what level of finished goods inventory you will need and when you will need to ship it.   This is normally done via a good sale projection in both units and dollars that you should be developing. Your manufacturing executive must have this information to properly support your launch.

Selling is a conversation with a purpose. Get to know the buyer as a person and as a consumer a little before you pitch them hard for an order. An experienced sale professional knows the value of relationship selling and that establishing this relationship is step one in a sales effort. In time your sales team will know which customers can easily be converted to a new product and which ones have some legacy loyalty to an existing competitive product. The important issue is to listen to your sales team, understand what they are dealing with and jointly develop solutions to enable them to penetrate and gain market share.

Next your product must meet the needs of your customers and long term no about of fancy footwork will change that. In the end the product with the best overall value wins.

Motivate your sales force to achieve the precise market penetration behavior you desire by structuring your sales compensation plan accordingly. Your sales team will have quarterly sales objectives, and your sales organization will be highly responsive to market activity, especially if this is a new product launch. Your competition will react to your new promotional activities or your product launch, so pay close attention to them, especially during this initial launch period. Based on feedback from the field, make appropriate adjustments in your tactical sales activities to ensure you achieve your sales objectives for each quarter and for the year. You can motivate your sales team in two ways, that is, compensation and recognition/respect, as follows:

Compensation. Keep in mind that the selling patterns of a sale representative usually will correlate to the sales incentive program. If the sales incentives for Product B are better than Product A, you will see more effort going towards Product B. Use the sales compensation systems to control and direct sale force behavior and priorities. A great sales incentive program attracts the best people and a consistently great sales compensation from year to year enables you to retain the very best sales professionals.

Recognition/Respect. One thing I learned from being in field sales is that people in the field are highly influenced by what home office people say and do when they are in the field. Sales representatives usually have an information link that goes from one rep to another and from the sales manager to the rep. It usually does not go beyond the sales manager to the regional manager and so on. Therefore, as the CEO, when you are with your field sales team make sure you are genuine and you say the things that need to be said to provide the team the confidence that we are winning and will continue to win this product war. Celebrate the success, recognize the special achievements, listen to the additional opportunities that can be exploited, listen to the challenges that exist in the field in a constructive manner. Too often the sales team can be criticized for whining or being negative. Don't go there; instead listen to the problems especially if a number of reps are saying the same thing. It is best if you are doing this in conjunction and in support with your sales and marketing executive. As CEO your job is to assist with making all company functions work smoothly in an effort to achieve your business objectives. Listen, learn, analyze, fix, and succeed. There is nothing more powerful and motivating to a sales force than to have real obstacles identified and understood that are quickly fixed by the executive team to enable more rapid sales expansion. This is the best way of showing respect for the men and women that work hard to sell your product everyday, and it is good for the company. If you do this successfully your sales team will talk about this for a very long time in a very positive manner. Again, your sales team will react to what they see and hear from you and less from the normal chain of command with all the filters that go with that.

Promotion Plan

If properly developed, your promotional plan involves a number of elements that are carefully designed to reinforce your sales message in the field. It is always important that the product messaging is consistent throughout all aspects of the sale and marketing materials. Your marketing executive is working closely with his/her brand managers, market research analysts, and sales management to provide a level of awareness and promotional events that are designed to reinforce the message of your sales representatives. Promotion programs are designed to supplement sales efforts, or create demand in area where so sales team is present. Depending on your product this promotional effort is a website, a portal, an email campaign, social networking, direct mail, TV, etc. Promotion, especially, electronic marketing is a fast moving ever-changing medium today that is powerful and requires effective management.

Production Plan

As you prepared for this launch months ago, you required your sales and manufacturing executives to jointly develop a launch plan that included a tactical sales forecast in sales and units. This forecast assumed a specific launch date and the manufacturing executive already produced the specific number of individual finished goods units required specified in the sales plan. Jointly with the two executives you instructed them to produce an addition 20% of finished good inventory just in case the launch was more successful than anticipate. This for now will be considered safety/contingent inventory for planning purposes and everyone hopes it will be needed. After several weeks and months of actual product sales, you will probably notice a shift in product mix and by sales channel. Work with sales to update the unit forecast, and shift production to meet the needs of sales as soon as possible. Change your raw material procurement schedule and production schedule, and shift certain production staff around to more optimally balance overall production to simultaneously deliver quality product to the field as needed within your normal product cost guidelines. Work closely with sales and marketing management to ensure you have the latest updates on unit sales projections to have the right product in the field at the right time to avoid any inventory back order situations. This is normal production planning and it is even more important that all the appropriate parties work together during the launch period to quickly react to all necessary changes. One thing you do not want at this time is a backorder situation. If initially have too much inventory then the manufacturing executive will slow down production to enable you to balance finished good inventory levels over the next few months. It is OK to be more flexible on inventory management and temporarily hold higher than normal inventory levels during launch periods, which by their very nature can be volatile and subject to big changes.

Working Capital

Months before when you prepared the launch plan your financial executive worked closely with your sales and manufacturing executive to develop a financial model to brought together the sales forecast, the staging of raw materials, work-in-process inventory, and finished goods inventory. This was possible because a sales forecast in sales dollars and units by month was prepared. This financial model was used to determine the working capital needs and the inventory purchase commitments were made several months ago. This financial forecast model also made certain assumptions for special payment discounts and delayed payment dating on initial product stocking orders that is a common practice. We have planned for the negative cash flow for this launch and anticipate that positive cash flow from delayed receivables will begin in 75 days from product shipments. It is important that you meet your anticipated launch plan sales target to avoid further cash challenges.

Product Development

You are fortunate to have this current product launch followed by an interesting line extension in six months. This will be motivating to your sales force and will help to strengthen relationships with your customers. Your plan anticipates that the line extension will incrementally increase your overall market share by 10 percent. The new line extension adds new your customers should readily accept features that your market research indicates. The unit forecast has been jointly prepared and you approved it just this week so production will begin immediately in the form of raw material purchases in time to easily meet the market launch timing six months from today. The cash flow forecast model reflects the cash requirement of this line extension launch and cash is sufficient to execute this launch plan.

Cash Flow

Your financial projection model shows that cash is sufficient if we meet our sales plan target. In the event there is a shortfall we are ready to reduce inventory levels and defer certain payments and expenditures to avoid a cash deficit. At least for now, you need to achieve your sales target to avoid cash problems later in the year.

Take away items

- <u>Partnering strategy</u>
  - You only get one chance to make a first impression
  - Preparation is 90% of the work involved in partnering
  - Before you are perceived as being professional you must be and look professional.
  - Your electronic data library and the construction of all the materials in this library reflect your integrity, attention to detail, and you knowledge of the partner's prospective with regard to what is need from this point forward

- Work hard to convince your prospective partners that you are an asset for them and not a future liability with the Agency (FDA).
- Fully integrated operating company (sales)
  - Know your markets and your customer needs better than anyone else
  - Stay close to your customers and listen to them, they really know what they want to buy.
  - Provide excellent customer care, and they will take care of you.
  - Never forget that marketing is warfare, the best side wins.
  - Stay on offense and do your best to keep you competitors on defense.
  - In the end the product that provides the customer with the best overall value wins. Determine early what attributes are for a successful product like improve your product to meet the market's needs.
  - Get the fundamentals right, build loyal market share by providing good value; take care of your customers, and the profits will follow.

CHAPTER 11

VALUE CREATION

Pressure makes diamonds
GEORGE S. PATTON

Understanding What and How Value is Created

Up to this point your efforts have been mostly devoted to preparation for something. That something has now arrived. Your company is now several years from those start up days. To date a number of very important accomplishments have been achieved as follows:

1. Patent Estate – You took that great idea and built a formidable patent estate around it that covers the key largest commercial markets of the world. Therefore, your coverage includes North America, Europe, Japan and other Asian and international markets that respect patents.
2. Capital Formation – You raised capital, but even more important you attracted high quality early investors that have assisted you in raising all the capital you needed to get to this point. Those high quality investors have a great reputation and add credibility to you and your company. They stand ready to help you with your next financing and your exit strategy when the time is right.
3. Business Strategy – You developed a winning business strategy and built your business around that strategy in a very focused, disciplined manner.

4. Management/Advisory Teams – You recruited a high quality team of operating executives, board members, advisors and consultants. This team has challenged your plans and thoughts, improved them, and helped you to avoid major mistakes.

5. Development Programs – You now have a number of development programs or late stage products if you plan to market products. Your development programs are at the point where partnering with key industry players is highly probable.

Your executive team joined your company because they believed in your great idea, and they believed in you and your ability to successfully lead this business to its full potential. They desired then, and continue to desire to use their talents to achieve something big that they can be part of. Your team is trained, they have made and learned from some mistakes, they are now more confident that every before and they are motivated to achieve greater challenges. Now is the time to exploit every ounce of those talents up and down the organization chart, the board room and the advisory teams to create real meaningful value for your shareholders, the latter that took a very substantial risk to fund you and your business.

Value can be created in several ways, to name a few:

1. Cash Flow – reasonably quantifiable annual future cash flows from operations. Reasonable people can attempt to project and quantify the probable result of future cash flows. Cash flow streams are critically important because they represent the basic fundamental factor in determining company value.

2. Motivated Acquisitions – sometimes a buyer will need to purchase an asset or a company in a hurry. This may be a defensive play or an offensive play on their part. In these situations, that buyer will often slightly overpay for an asset that fits their needs. Overpay means that they may consider paying a little more than the value of projected annual cash flows. The buyer may need your patents, your technology pipeline, your trade secrets, facilities, or your partnership agreements for their own strategic

purpose. This is the kind of opportunity that may periodically present to a lucky company. You cannot plan or count on such an outcome, but it is great if you should be blessed by motivated acquisition.

3. Capabilities/Other Assets – A buyer may be very interested in obtaining your sales force or your manufacturing facility and manufacturing team. The acquisition of your teams may buy them time in the marketplace and fill both a tactical and strategic need that has substantial value to them.

4. The Present Value of Future Cash Flows – This is often what all your years of effort and achievement condense to. It is one number prepared by a financial analyst/investment banker with such skills. That person gets the privilege of quantifying the value of the projected annual cash flows that you receive from your corporate partners. It would include up front payments, milestone payments, approval payments and ongoing royalties on sales to their customers. The same would apply to operating profits from a fully integrated operating company, if that is your chosen strategy

Concept of Present Value Analysis

If you are going to be measured by future cash flows it is best to learn a little about this concept if you are not already familiar with it. This necessarily involves numbers and some detail so bear with me on this section as I try to make my point.

One can better understand the concept of present value by attempting to answer the following question:

Would you prefer to take $10,000 today or $1,750 annually for 8 years?

Now there may be a pressing reason why you need the $10,000 today but for the purpose of this analysis let's ignore that issue and take the approach that you are indifferent to the payment choice, as you do not have an immediate pressing cash flow challenge. Your really need to think about which chose is better and there are quantitative techniques that can help you with this decision.

Accepting cash up front - Having said this there are several important factors to consider when accepting full payment up front, such as:

- Collection risk. There is no collection risk involving future payments
- Interest rates. There is no need to worry about interest rates of the time value of money
- Performance risk. There is no performance risk related to the level of future cash flows
- $10,000 has it benefits but you could be leaving money on the table

Normally accepting a future stream of cash flows requires the consideration of a number of factors, such as:

- Will the party that will be generating the projected cash flows do better or worse than the projection? Did they hedge their forecast, or did they provide you the optimistic sales version? What does your own analysis tell you? Payment risk. Is their any payment risk? Does the other party have debt, legal disputes, and competitive challenges ahead of them? Could something very bad occur, or are they in a position to really let it rip and capture high levels of market share?
- Time value of money. This is especially important with cash flows that occur over many years. What is the time value of money if that cash were deployed into another business need or new venture? What if interest rates rise or fall dramatically over time?
- Projection reliability. While this does not really apply when there is a fixed payment schedule it would make a difference on contingent milestone or royalty on sales payments, so remember this concept.
- Bankable cash flow. Is the cash flow coming from a party that is considered a good credit risk and a capable industry payer? Will

a bank or other lending institution provide a loan to your company now, in whole or in part, based on the projected cash flow of your new technology deal?

The above are some subjective considerations for a quantifiable financial calculation. However, this is the real world of business that does not always offer clear lines and hard cold facts to work with. I often say that a CEO must be comfortable with managing gray as there are few situations that are simply just black and white.

Now let's do a basic standard discounted cash flow financial calculation to the original question of taking $10,000 today vs. $1,750 annually for eight years. In this example by adding up the annual discounted cash flows you will be able to determine the net present value of the multi-year payment stream. Now to do this I have to use an interest rate (discount factor) in order to quantify the time value of money. In this case I will use 5% interest rate and another alternative that I will call a discount factors. Now if I were concerned about execution risk or payment risk I would increase the discount factor to 15% or 25%, possibly more. However, let's not get too carried away and just assume there is no payment or execution risk and a 5% discount factor is fair and reasonable but you want to also consider a 10% discount factor simply due to the opportunity cost of that cash. There are many sophisticated methods for determining net present value or discounted cash flow, but this basic illustration is provided to present the concept.

Disc. Rate Used	Net Present Value	NET PRESENT VALUE CONCEPT							
		Y E A R							
		1	2	3	4	5	6	7	8
Payment Stream		$1,775	1,775	1,775	1,775	1,775	1,775	1,775	1,775
5%		0.950	0.903	0.857	0.815	0.774	0.735	0.698	0.663
	$11,351	$1,686	1,602	1,522	1,446	1,373	1,305	1,240	1,178
10%		0.900	0.810	0.729	0.656	0.590	0.531	0.478	0.430
	$9,098	$1,598	1,438	1,294	1,165	1,048	943	849	764

The above table suggests that the discounted cash flow of eight annual payments results in a total net present value of $11,351 at a 5% discount rate, and $9,098 at a 10% discount rate. Please observe the following:

- The annual payments are discounted for time each year under for both discount rates.
- The net present value is the sum of the discounted annual payment streams. Notice
- The annual discounted cash flow show the impact of higher discounted in each successive year. For example, the discount factor used in year 8 is .663 (66%) vs. .95 (5%) in year one. Technically the first payment should not be discounted since it would normally be an up front payment. However, I chose to assume an end of year payment to amplify the discounting process.

If you are satisfied with a 5% discount factor then the 8-year payment stream is your best choice. The 5% discount rate clearly calculates to a net present value above $10,000; while the other, the 10% discount rate, clearly calculates to a result below $10,000. Therefore, the choice depends on the cost of money assumptions you choose make to determine what alternative is best for you.

Now, to bring this home a little, apply this concept to a royalty stream on a partnering deal. We will discuss this in more detail in a later chapter.

Value Creation by Type of Business Strategy

Depending on the type of company you choose, value creation opportunities may differ, as follows:

1. For a Development Company

Your development programs have progressed to a point of maturation necessary to enable corporate partnering. Often the years your team has developed and brought forward a number of interesting programs all of which are available for partnering, as planned.

You were wise to recruit a seasoned business development executive what has been preparing materials and soliciting partners for several months. The executive was careful to first understand the strategic needs of prospective partners and targeted the right group for each of your programs. In some cases a partner has interest in more than one program. You are currently engaged with several prospective partners on multiple projects from the early discuss stage to negotiation stage.

Product A. Last month you concluded your first partnering deal for Product A. This deal took six months to complete all the due diligence from the first face-to-face meeting. This deal reflected the quality efforts of your entire management team in preparing a high quality, easy to access electronic library of all key material agreements, preclinical studies, chemistry and manufacturing data, regulatory reviews, patent estate matters and all other information concerning Product A. Two months ago your development executive's team completed a Phase I clinical trial with good safety results, and also prepared a detailed Phase II program. The deal terms include a $1 million up front payment, the potential for contingent milestone payments totaling $1.5 million over time based on the achievement of additional development objectives, a success fee of $1.5 million on FDA approval, and a 8.0% royalty on net sales for the life of all valid patents in all countries. This partnering deal was widely reported, involved a respected large Big Pharma A company, and has established a great deal of credibility for this program and may offer additional credibility for the other programs in your pipeline. Product A has the potential to achieve between $500 Million and $1 Billion in total annual global sales with approval anticipated in four years.

Product B. Your have been in discussions with two partners for four months and so far the discussions are going very well. The recently announced deal with Big Pharma A increased credibility and increases the probability of a deal eventually concluding on Product B with one of the two parties. You will continue to respectfully work with both parties but you are now at the point in the discussions where some level of commitment is warranted from one or both of those companies. Out of courtesy, you have informed both parties that they are not alone in discussions concerning Product B. Since the recent deal announcement with Big Pharma A, both companies have requested the next meeting and meeting dates are set. So far no major partnering objections are remaining and the due diligence process is nearing completion. The due diligence process on Product B went faster due to improvements made last year in the electronic library. These improvements were the result of issues encountered with due diligence efforts on Product A during discussions with BigPharma A. An improved electronic library system has now made it easier and faster to complete the partnering due diligence process. You anticipate that the next meetings with both parties will involve a discussion of possible deal structures and terms. You and your Business Development executive are preparing internal term sheet and deal strategies to prepare for those upcoming meetings.

Product C. Four parties have expressed early interest in Product C and recently after the deal announcement; two more parties have solicited you for information to begin the process. Your business development executive has schedule a number of meetings at your and at the targets locations and meeting preparations are in progress.

Product D. Your development team is ready to take Product D into the clinic with a Phase I trial. The IND (Investigational New Drug application) should be filed by next Friday and unless the FDA objects you plan to begin the Phase I study 30 days from the date of the IND submission. The signing payment from the Product A deal will come in handy to supplement the cost of the Phase I study.

2. For a Fully-Integrated Operating Company

You are actively selling one or more products and planning to launch additional products and line extensions of existing products in the future. Your business focus is on product sales, customer satisfaction, market research, competitive intelligence, market share penetration, pricing, medical reimbursement, manufacturing, distribution, inventory management, working capital management, cash flow, and earnings per share. You receive weekly sales reports from your financial team and pay close attention to what is happening in the field with customers and your competitors. You are simultaneously playing offense and defense at all times and it must be working because sales continue to rise. You have a product development team that is working on preparing new products and also line extensions of existing products. Your financial projection model reflects planned launch dates, manufacturing ramp ups for new product entries, a launch budget for sales and marketing, and a cash flow forecast that identifies your cash challenges for at least the next 12 months, by month. Your plan calls for the company to turn its first profit in four months and you are working very hard to make that happen. Now, how you build value with this business model is with earnings. Along the way you will celebrate sales growth and positive customer feedback as great success stories. However, at the end of the day what really matters in building company value is reliable cash flow and earnings per share. Consider that a stream or royalties is really no different than a stream of operating profit/cash flow. Not to get too technical, but there is a difference between operating profit and cash flow. The reconciling differences between the two are usually working capital, changes in long-term debt, and capital expenditures, none of which are reflected directly in operating profit. It is important to note that true cash flow can either be greater to less than operating profit. If it is greater, it is a selling point, if not don't even mention it.

So now you have a product or two on the market and the resources to build those products. Your company is cash flow stable, your teams are in place, and now it is time to go to higher levels. Higher sales and operating profits levels should lead to higher cash flow, which should then lead to a higher company valuation. It is the CEO's job to constantly engage in activities that increase shareholder value and higher profits can always be counted on as a good objective.

Expanding your product offerings

Consider developing additional products and line extensions. However, you may be near the end of what additional products can come out of that initial program. Consider the following when attempting to reach out to build company value:

- Constantly look for new product opportunities and strongly encourage your team to also do so. One of the best ways to find good new product opportunities is to analyze markets and determine what the market needs that is currently missing in that market. Find the market needs and voids and fill them with new products from your company.

- Depending on your level of interest and your timing it may be advisable to recruit an experienced new products executive to accelerate achievements in securing new product opportunities. A dedicated full-time executive whose only responsibility is to find and obtain new product opportunities to grow the company best handles this function.

- There may be a need in the market that can be exploited by obtaining a certain product from another company that does not see or choose to take advantage filling a void. It may be an older or out of favor product to that company. Consider buying that product from that company and plugging into your product development team and sales force.

- Acquire a non-core division of a larger company or another company whose product line is complementary to yours. There are always reasons why a company may sell a division or a line with one reason being that they recently decided to refocus their business. Yes, this can be a bold move but executed properly, intelligent, accretive (friendly to earnings per share) acquisitions can be a great way to quickly build operating scale and revenues. If you can make the difficult decisions to reduce redundant overhead, such a move can lead to a strong increase in earnings per share and cash flow.

Other value creation assets and programs

Development. As you moved your development programs along you built a strong development team. In order to achieve all this you constructed an outstanding development center with labs, a vivarium for animal testing, and a special infectious disease containment lab for one of your key programs. Six months ago, you completed and validated your pilot GMP (Good Manufacturing Practices) manufacturing facility to support the production of your active ingredients and your clinical supplies. The clinical supplies just manufactured in your GMP facility were used for your Phase I trial for Product A and will be used for the Phase I trial for Product B. All of the above are valuable assets that have great value not only to you but also to another company that wishes to jump start much of their development work infrastructure to race products to market. Be careful not to ignore this asset as this is now a turnkey operation that has real value to the right buyer.

Sales Force. If you are a sales company you already established a successful, operating sales force. This sales force is now operating in the field and knows its customer base very well. District and regional management systems are in place. Finally the administrative support for the field team and the senior sales executive are on board. Everyone is doing their job and ready to take on additional products should then become available. Your sales force is a valuable asset that should not be ignored. Your sales force can be especially valuable to a company that just obtained a product and need a sales force to sell it.

Cost reduction programs

Another way to increase cash flow and earnings per share are cost reduction programs. There are always opportunities to shave a few expenses if you take the time to look for them. It is always best to include cost improvement programs as one of your operating objectives within in each functional area. Volume-based raw material procurement programs, labor saving processes, high capacity equipment purchases that requires fewer labor hours. Build such things into your culture.

Let me offer you one example of a cost improvement program I was involved with years ago. I was observing that the plastic caps on the bottles of two of our largest SKU's (stock keeping units – bottles) were identical except for color, with one being white and the other red. I checked around and determined that there was no compelling reason why two colors were necessary especially since both bottles sat on a pharmacy shelf and had no contact with the end using customers. After further analysis it was determined that if we simply switch the red cap to white it would result in an annual savings of $250,000 annually because of a larger volume discount. Who knew? For this I received a special bonus and special personal congratulations from the CEO. It was effortless and the opportunity was right in front our noses! So capture the low hanging cost reduction fruit when you can. Apply that incremental annual cash flow to a present value model and it is now worth millions instead of just $250,000. In the process of building value sometimes you have to think like an investment banker.

Much good is happening at all levels of the company and you are and should be pleased. This is what you planned and worked hard for, wanted to do all along, and now you are right in the middle of the arena. Exploit every opportunity you can, maximize the value of your teams and technology. You are a gladiator and it is you time in the arena – go for it!

Investment Banking
This morning you received a call from an investment banker. You were in a meeting when he called. You will soon find out that the investment banker is soliciting you based on the recently announced partnering deal with BigPharma A. Should this be of interest to you this is one of the first events on this subject. Any deal that may come out of this will take months to complete. As you know, your long-term exit strategy calls for one of the exit options to be an IPO.

Earlier in the week your lead early venture investor reached out to a high quality investment-banking firm to consider an IPO of your company. The lead venture investor and this banking firm have done six successful deals together in the past four years. More work and further validation of your technology will be required, but the idea is attractive to both sides. A second technology partnering deal will go a long way in convincing the investment banking community that there is real technology here that is in demand by quality industry players. The partnering deal terms, especially the ongoing royalty and the protected market life provided by your strong patent estate, will drive the pre-money valuation that the investment bankers will support for the anticipated IPO pricing. These investment banking deals take time and require SEC review, and intense road shows to investor groups. It is also possible that a partnering deal with Product B may even be concluded by the time the IPO is declared effective by the SEC.

Take away issues

- Your entire team needs to perform at their best levels during this stage more than at any other time in the company's history
- This is when the training, the operating efficiency, and the teamwork you have worked so hard to achieve pays off
- This is the stage that increases the value of equity of all involved. Remind everyone of that fact as they need to work the hardest they have to date with your company
- Lever lose focus on the most important value creation opportunities and take the time to communicate those priorities to your executive often to enable them to also remain in focus
- This is the stage where you and your team are building equity value for your shareholders and your families.

CHAPTER 12

THE EXIT PHASE

*Your technology is only worth what
others are willing to pay for it.*

Preparing Your Due Diligence Package

Your exit opportunity may present itself in various forms, so your thinking should always remain flexible on this matter. Timing, risk, near-term value, and tax implications will often be considerations in exit transactions, which is why you need to be working with professions that can provide you proper guidance on such an important transaction.

Disclosure Documents

In chapter 8 The Commercialization Phase, we discussed technical due diligence regarding your products and technologies. In chapter 4 ("Funding / Capital Formation"), we discussed the need for a PPM and later an S-1 (and at a later stage, follow-on SEC registration filings). All of these documents are disclosure statements, and in an exit you should anticipate needing to update all such disclosure documents to make them current and to disclose the material aspects of the exit deal in whatever form it comes. If at the time of an exit transaction, you are already a publicly trading company, much of this will already be reasonably current, so updates are required. If you are not public, most likely you will take your last PPM and update it to make it current. As always, you should keep these documents well organized and complete to maintain your credibility with the other party and to facilitate their very detailed review.

Electronic Data Library

You will want to update your electronic data library for all product and technical matters, but also for all corporate disclosure matters. The library should contain executed versions of all material contracts, all financial statements issued, audit reports, insurance contracts, employment agreements, board and committee minutes, lease obligations, loans, convertible securities, equity contracts, and the contracts of all derivatives involving company stock, stock options, warrants, and convertible debt instruments.

Due Diligence Completion

As discussed earlier due diligence will be complete when all the objections have been handled to the satisfaction of both parties. This will take time, effort, and good people skills to make it happen successfully.

Negotiating the Exit Deal

Yes, deals involve both form and valuation. The form will be the required due diligence and the mounds of paperwork and legal requirements that enable a deal to close and money change hands. We will cover form, but initially I wish to focus on valuation, that is the determination of the value of your company should be sold for.

Value Determination

Consistent, reliable cash flow streams from quality industry players will ultimately provide a base valuation for your company. This effort will initially involve a fair amount of quantitative analysis. However, in the end your company will only be worth what another party is willing to pay for it. With that stated, understand negotiating complex technology partnering deals is both an art and science.

Negotiating is a controlled argument between two opposing parties. Notice I did not refer to them as enemies and that is because they need to work closely with each other going forward in an effort to achieve a common objective. A successful, constructive, negotiating phase requires that each party fights for their team to get the best deal for their company. The parties need to agree on a fair compensation. They also need to craft an agreement that encourages each party to work closely and constructively with each other to achieve a common objective. In the end what each party want is a successful product approval resulting in maximizing sales of that product in the marketplace.

So how does one negotiate such a deal?

Let's answer that question with an exit case study. Deals can take many structures and an entire book could be written on such matters. For this purpose of this book the case study below will touch upon many of the features and challenges one needs to address and successfully conclude to close a deal. I hope you find this case study useful in understanding what is required to negotiate and close a deal with this structure.

Negotiation Style.
Combative negotiation interactions generally fail or do not produce good lasting deals. A good deal is really a "win-win" deal for both sides. In your negotiations you wish to achieve a certain product outcome, and financial rewards for that outcome. The other side takes the substantial financial risk and both parties need to work together to achieve success. To quote the definition of the word **argument** from Wikipedia

*In logic and philosophy, an **argument** is a series of statements typically used to persuade someone of something or to present reasons for accepting a conclusion.* [1][2] *The general form of an argument in a natural language is that of premises (typically in the form of propositions, statements or sentences) in support of a claim: the conclusion.*[3][4][5] *The structure of some arguments can also be set out*

in a formal language, and formally defined "arguments" can be made indepen-
dently of natural language arguments, as in math, logic, and computer science.

It is always useful to use persuasive arguments to achieve a certain outcome in negotiations. People generally respect a good, well developed argument and, if so, are more inclined to accept it. Consider spending less time providing or reacting to macho statements and more time preparing thoughtful persuasive arguments. If you follow this advice you may find that your negotiations might be more productive and may often lead to a better post deal relationship with the other party.

Deal Structure.

First lets outline the overall structure of this acquisition deal. Buyer A wishes to acquire 100% of the stock of your company. The proposal calls for payment to be made 50% in cash and 50% in common stock of Buyer A, a large publicly traded company that is listed on the New York Stock Exchange. The entire payment to your shareholders will take place at the closing of the deal with shareholders receiving both cash and shares of Buyer A held in escrow for fast distribution to all shareholders within 15 days of the closing. Buyer A intends to retain no less than 90%, and possibly more, of the current number of employees in your company. In general, this is a simple deal structure with no unusual, exotic deal features.

Know your Buyer's Needs, Wants and Fears - Who is Buyer A and what is their motivation for doing this deal?

Buyer XYZ – The Proposed Acquirer of the ABC Biotech Company

Buyer XYZ is a sales company that wishes to strategically grow its worldwide business by developing and obtaining approval for new products to market as their worldwide brands. Recently they licensed four new technologies from different companies and are planning development activities. However Buyer A does not have a development infrastructure to successfully develop its programs. They can either build that development function over time or acquire one. Buyer A does not have an interest in both Products A and B for their own global development. However, they would like to have the partnering cash flow that may come with those deals to improve their future earnings per share. Buyer A is highly motivated to acquire your Product C and Product D as well as your entire preclinical pipeline. Buying your company and its development infrastructure will add quality product opportunities and enable Buyer A to jump start its development activities to enable them to race more products to market faster than if they were to build their own development infrastructure.

What Buyer A gets in the deal.

By purchasing 100% of your companies stock, Buyer A receives the following:

1. Product A - The potential cash flow from the partnering deal on Product A to include all milestone payments, approval success fees, and finally the entire future royalty stream on sales to customers.
2. Product B – The rights to Product B, however, they would prefer to partner this program because it's therapeutic focus is not consistent with Buyer A's strategic plan. If Product B is partnered, Buyer A will receive 100% of the cash flow of that deal to include the upfront payment, milestone payments, approval success fees, and finally the entire royalty stream on sales to customers.
3. Product C – the rights to this program worldwide. While this can be partnered, Buyer A wishes to keep this program and develop it to be a core product in their global product sales effort.
4. Product D – the rights to this program that will soon enter Phase I clinical trials. Again, while this program can be partnered, Buyer A wishes to keep this program and develop it to be a core product in their global product sales effort.
5. Preclinical pipeline. Your preclinical pipeline consists of six promising leads all of which fit the strategic plan of Buyer A
6. Your corporate assets and liabilities include:

a. Cash and any receivables amounting to approximately $10 million
b. Your entire patent estate
c. Your development facility and all the assets within it.
d. Your outstanding balance sheet liabilities totaling less than $500,000
e. Most of your employees. Buyer A anticipates that they will keep no less than 90%, and possibly more, of the current number of employees post acquisition.
f. Severance liability incurred in the transaction amounting to $500,000 or less depending on the severity of the severance program.

What are your needs, wants and fears?

You and your team have been working extremely hard for years. You have created some significant value with more value creation in the works. If you can negotiate a great deal for your shareholders now with certainty, you should consider doing it. If the deal is not right, you can continue doing building you company. If you don't do this deal you will still be running your show the way you want. If you do the deal your shareholders will be happy, and almost all your employees will be able keep their positions. Some of your administrative people will remain but others will be declared redundant. to include yourself as a CEO. When your board approved your employment agreement they wanted to make it easier and worth your while to accept sacrificing your CEO job in an acquisition that would be good for all shareholders. That severance package now shows a significant payout that is intended to sooth any emotional wounds you may have.

Buyer XYZ may have an ongoing operational role for you personally in the combined company that does not include being the CEO of Buyer XYZ. They may also wish to have you on retainer for 1-2 years to help with the transition. In the event you do no have an operating role with the new company, the outstanding success of this deal will make it very easy for you to do another deal right after this one as long as that does not compete with Buyer A. If so, enjoy a little time off and your newfound wealth for a short period of time before you start your search for your next deal. You will not be surprised if people begin to call you to lead a new deals given the success of this deal

Acquisition Price.

So how does one negotiate the price of a deal like this?

Verbal and non-verbal communication

First, remember this always. When involved in negotiations anything you say can and will be held against you. That means everything you may say in a cab, over dinner, at a ballgame, in an airport, in an email, or over the telephone, or to another lower level member of the opposing team is just like saying it inside a conference room. Consider everything you say and do to be recorded so keep your guard at all times and make sure your team does the same. To use a great quote from the Godfather – "Never let anyone outside the family know what you are thinking". Also remember that often it is the non-verbal communication that can hurt you so be careful about how you manage non-verbal communication. As always a good poker face works because nobody can read your mind. Therefore, if you don't say anything, or send non-verbal communication, the other side has absolutely no idea what you are thinking. That is what you want most of the time.

Break down a complicated deal into smaller parts

Yes, determining value can be a difficult task so as you do with all other things that are difficult break down a big task into smaller, more manageable components. After you break it down just analyze each component one at a time and then add them up to get a value. You have done this in the past it just has been with other topics.

Earlier we discussed making arguments and it is useful and better to negotiate with logical arguments vs. emotion. Emotions will inevitably enter into the discussions and you will need to learn how to deal with emotions, or use emotions to your advantage. However, arguments, in my opinion, are what move negotiations forward constructively and can be respected as discussion points even if the other party chooses not to agree with your argument in your presence. Let's consider both issues, as follows:

Logical arguments

Let's build this house one brick at a time. By that I mean let's identify all assets and liabilities in this deal and attempt to quantify each component in a logical, quantifiable, building block approach. This will take a little preparation but your team can and should be working with these value models long before the first negotiating session.

Buyer A

Product A – The beauty of the Product A deal is that it has closed and the partner is a major industry player, which means that the potential cash flow from this deal needs to be take seriously. The first item you need to complete is a carefully developed financial projection model that projects sales anticipated approval dates and projected licensing payments and royalty payments. The two parties will not agree on the level of sales or timing of approval but make sure you accurately quantify the deal and its structure to make sure there are no misunderstandings on the basics of the deal itself. While I would place one version of the financial projection in the electronic library, I would also run alternate scenarios to better appreciate the financial impact of higher or lower sales (and royalties) and perhaps a delayed approval launch. Buyer A will be doing this for sure do be prepared. By doing all this you have built the argument for a discounted cash flow value for Product A, subject to discussion. Agree on the structure of the analysis and argue the assumptions to some point of agreement and then use the model to quantify the net present value of that asset. It is fair to put a reasonable discount on this or any other program that does not enjoy regulatory approval.

Your challenge is to make the arguments that reduce the risk factors and therefore minimize deep discounting of the projected cash flows

Product B – You are now motivated to close an agreement for Product B because a closed deal is worth a lot more than a possible deal. You will still need to prepare you best estimate of what that deal might look at to include the sales projection that are anticipated. Your approach to defining a value can and should be performed in the same way the value for Product A was determined. However, any projections will be subject to much higher discount factors unless a deal is consummated before the acquisition is consummated.

Products C and D – Buyer A wishes to keep these programs for its own use on a global basis. It would be logical to craft a hypothetical partnering deal bases on the deal structures of Product A and hopefully Product B. I would use these projections as arguments of value creation in the negotiations. It is difficult to quantify a value for these programs but basing value of these programs on other closed deals in a reasonable argument that should be respected. Generally, in negotiating any deal it is best to offer respectable arguments that are logical and make sense as opposed to macho emotions demands that can just slow down a good deal and create unnecessary conflict between the negotiating teams

The preclinical pipeline

This asset has value but it is early, with a high risk factor and should and will be heavily discounted by Buyer A. Your challenge is to make the arguments that reduce risk and sell the potential efficacy of these programs.

Development facility and other assets.

Forget what is on the balance sheet for these assets. Prepare an analysis that defines the replacement cost of such a facility. To this add the cost and time of recruiting the entire development team as will as building the facility itself. Finally, add to this the opportunity cost involved if Buyer A builds their own facility over a period of one to two years. Buyer

A will not admit that they agree with anything you present in this analysis. However, I assure you they will use it to present such an argument to their own management in later stage reviews of the negotiations at Buyer A's senior management levels.

Balance sheet
Your balance sheet has cash, receivables and some liabilities. This will most likely be a relatively small amount compared to the total acquisition price. Nevertheless, make sure you place the balance sheet assets on the list and not just give them away.

It is best to prepare and/or to negotiate the details of this deal as described above. However, keep in mind that at the end of the day Buyer A will simply declare that based on their analysis they are only willing to accept an acquisition price of something like $250 million dollars. Often deals come down to this, a simple number that you can take or leave.

Risk factors to consider
You operate in a high risk/high reward industry environment. Just because your recently partnered your Product A does not guarantee that you will every receive one dollar of royalties. The product could fail in the pivotal trials, develop a safety problem, fail to achieve acceptable labeling from the FDA to maximize its sales potential, or just simply fail in the marketplace versus other competitive entries. These are all high risk factors that reasonable people will use to discount multiple years of cash flow stream that involve millions of dollars in royalty payments.

Making the last very difficult decision
In the final stages of the negotiations be prepared to know what your lowest acceptable number is to sell out, at this time. However, be flexible because too often management teams of development companies start to believe their own spin only to later find out that their own perceptions of value were too high. You have many risk factors ahead of you and a number of things

can go wrong to offset your optimism. Remember, your company is only worth what others are willing to pay for it. It is possible that the proposed acquisition price may be considered reasonable but low, in your opinion. Given the magnitude of this decision it is really not yours to make, or even the board of directors, but instead all the shareholders as a group. Any reasonable acquisition offer should be put to a shareholder vote so they can decide as they have taken the risk. If you strongly disagree with the deal you can offer your opinion as well as the support for your opinion in the shareholder proxy statement. You or your board can even recommend not taking the deal. Your shareholders will appreciate your opinion, they may be confused and ask questions, but in the end they will decide for themselves on what this deal means to them, at this time. Major decisions like this are legally and morally reserved for a full shareholder vote.

Let's Consider Ways to Quantify The Acquisition of the ABC Biotech Company by Buyer XYZ.

In completing this quantitative analysis of the ABC Biotech Company we will consider the following:

1. The four development programs with special emphasis on Program A that has already been partnered with BigPharma A.
2. The preclinical pipeline
3. The development facilities and development team
4. The patent estate's value beyond the current pipeline
5. Balance sheet assets and liabilities

Product A

Quantifying the Net Present Value Arguments for Program BigPharma A. In this analysis we will do the following:

1. List the key agreement terms
2. Prepare/review cash flow projections of the Program A
3. Calculate several Net Present Value scenarios of the cash flow projections

Key Terms of the Product A Agreement

1. Signature payment (received) - payable on the final execution of the partnering/licensing agreement with all necessary approvals.
2. Contingent milestone payments:
   a. $ 250,000 – start of any phase II clinical program
   b. $ 500,000 – start of any phase III clinical program
   c. $ 750,000 – filing of the NDA (New Drug Application)
   d. $ 1,500,000 – FDA approval payment
   e. Total payments of $3,000,000 (contingent, not guaranteed)
3. Royalty on sales to customers of 8.0% of Net Sales to be paid as follows:
   a. On all sales to customers
   b. For as long as there is at least one valid patent (has not expired) in each territory (country/region)
   c. In all territories of the world
   d. Royalty payments stops after patent expire in each territory

Financial Projection Model –

1. The financial impact of the deals terms can be further analyzed in table.
2. This table projects net sales of Product A with input from BigPharma A.
3. The table also reflects the timing of key milestone achievements and launch date as projected with input from BigPharma A.
4. The appropriate royalty rates are applied to the sales projection.
5. The model provides a Net Present Value Calculation to aid in the negotiation process. For discussion purposes there are two deal timing scenarios:
   a. The first scenario that assumes the exit deal is done now

b. The second scenario assumes that the ABC Biotech Company decides to delay the exit deal for two years and to take the chance for a higher return.

6. All NPV values are provided using discount factors of 20, 25, 30, 35, and 40% to aid in the negotiating discussions.

Net Present Value Analysis – based on the following assumptions

1. Market years – these represent the years Product A will be sold by BigPharma A and be protected by the first set of valid patents. After projecting for the completion of all development work, NDA filing, a FDA approval review time BigPharma A is expecting to enjoy six years of market exclusivity before the first patents expire.

2. Patent protected extension years –
    a. What Are They - the astute management of the ABC Biotech was wise enough to invest in additional post initial patent filing research and development activities. They were also able to broaden and tighten their initial patents to make them more attractive to corporate partners. In the course of doing this additional work they were able to discover new inventions and/or improvements that were novel and not obvious, a requirement for patent prosecution. Additional patents for these new novel, not obvious, improvements were filed, and patents were granted.
    b. What is the Benefit - As a result of the additional patent filings the market life of Product A, was extended by three additional years, now for a total of nine market years. It cost less than $50,000 to do the research/development work and file the patents during the early development stage. The benefit is that the royalty stream paid by BigPharma A is now extended three more years, that represent the best sales years, adding significantly to the Net Present Value of the Product A partnering deal

NET PRESENT VALUE ANALYSIS

Contract Signature	1	2	3	4	5	6	7	8	9	10	11	12	13
PROTECTED YEARS OF PRODUCT MARKETING													
Payments			ORIGINAL LIFE OF FIRST INVENTION PATENTS								PATENT LIFE EXTENSIONS		
In Thousands of Dollars													
CLINICAL STUDIES & REGULATORY APPROVALS													
Projected Product A Sales													
North America	40,000				100,000	150,000	200,000	250,000	300,000	350,000	400,000	450,000	450,000
Europe					20,000	50,000	75,000	100,000	125,000	150,000	175,000	200,000	225,000
Japan					20,000	50,000	75,000	100,000	125,000	150,000	175,000	200,000	225,000
Other					10,000	25,000	37,500	50,000	62,500	75,000	85,000	95,000	100,000
Worldwide Total	**40,000**				**150,000**	**275,000**	**387,500**	**500,000**	**612,500**	**725,000**	**835,000**	**945,000**	**1,000,000**
Partnering Payments		Ph II	Ph III	File	Approval								
Milestones		250	500	750	1,500						-	-	
Royalties 8.0%	-	-	-	-	12,000	22,000	31,000	40,000	49,000	58,000	66,800	75,600	80,000
Total Payments		**250**	**500**	**750**	**13,500**	**22,000**	**31,000**	**40,000**	**49,000**	**58,000**	**66,800**	**75,600**	**80,000**

NPV calculated to begin in year one

NPV			Patent Extension Value	
Rate	10 Years	7 Years	3 Years	
20%	90,459	60,523	29,936	
25%	65,327	46,163	19,164	
30%	48,253	35,755	12,498	
35%	36,377	28,087	8,291	
40%	27,938	22,351	5,587	

If You Waited 2 Years — NPV calculated as if the deal was completed in year three instead of now

	2 Years	Patent Extension Value	
20%	$129,461	$86,353	$43,108
25%	$101,261	$71,317	$29,944
30%	$80,722	$59,601	$21,121
35%	$65,460	$50,350	$15,110
40%	$53,909	$42,958	$10,951

Review and Analysis

From the above analysis allow me to point out the following for your review:

1. Timelines –
   a. Four additional years of development and approval time is projected before any sales of Product A can be achieved.
   b. The primary period of market exclusivity (all territories) is projected to be seven years
   c. The second set of patents adds three additional sales years, and at the highest sales levels
2. Milestone Payments – contingent payments ($3 million total) based on the achievement of the following milestones
   a. Planning year two achievement - $250,000
   b. Planning year three achievement - $500,000
   c. Planning year four achievement - $750,000
   d. FDA approval - $1,500,000
3. Product Sales – all sales dollars reflected in ($ 000's)
   a. Territories – North America (US, Canada, Mexico), Europe, Japan, All Other – ROW (rest of world)
   b. Regulatory approvals – US approval is anticipated first, then Europe and others a year later
   c. All sales reflected in US dollar equivalent beginning with $40 million in from North America in year one, and with peak annual sales of $1 Billion worldwide
   d. All sales and timing for the purposed of this analysis are considered to be reasonable, but subject to negotiation
4. Royalty on Sales - 8.0%
5. Discount Factors –
   a. Five alternative discount rates were presented for further analysis
   b. DCF is present for all years, only the first seven years (first patents), and the patent life extension period of three years)

Narrative/Overview

Quick Overview
Based on the assumptions used in the Product A financial projection and a discount factor of 30% the Net Present Value of Product A for the purpose of valuing this asset for acquisition is approximately $48 million.

A Few Incoming Arguments You Should Be Anticipating From the Buyer A's Negotiating Team
General - Remember that Buyer A's negotiating team is being paid to get the best price for their company. Product A is only one of the assets they are buying. They will make a long list of concerns and objections and put doubt in your mind as to the real value of Product A to include all the associated risks inherent in any risky drug development program. They may even tell you that it may not be worth anything because it may never get approved if a safety problem in uncovered in later stage clinical trials. You will come prepared for all the arguments you anticipate they will make, understanding that they really mean some of them and the others are for negotiating leverage. In time you might be able to determine which objections are real or not. For now you must treat all objections as real and make the argument against them. By the way there are few right and wrong answers here. This is the art involved in negotiating deals. It is making arguments for items whose value cannot be definitively quantified and verified like a bank cash balance. Below is a list of some of the arguments you should anticipate.

- Launch date:
  - The combination of additional development time and regulatory review time should be at least five years instead of four.
  - This will delay the launch and reduce and delay the royalty payout.
- Sales Dollar & Units Forecast:

- The price BigPharma A has assumed is too high and will not be accepted by all medical insurance carriers
- The market penetration rates of Product A are too high in all territories and the growth rates are not reasonable
- The prices in Europe and Japan will be lower than the US
- Regulatory Approval:
  - Key markets such as Europe and Japan will not follow until 18 months later on after the US, not 12 months
  - The All Other (ROW) territory projection is too soon, too high and the prices will have to be much lower to be accepted in poorer countries
- Discount Rate:
  - The discount rate of only 20% is way too low and does not adequately reflect the real risk involved in such risky drug development programs.
  - A higher rate of 40% would be a more appropriate discount rate on a high-risk program like Product A.

A Few Arguments You Will Be Making to Buyer A's Negotiating Team

General – Obviously, you are negotiating to get the best overall deal for the ABC Biotech Company. Keep in mind that negotiation is both an art and a science. You need to make both business and technical arguments (science) and you need to present and sell them effectively (art) to the other party.

Buyer A, from what you know, has a very good reason to acquire your company and it is not just for the development team and facility. They are attracted to your pipeline because it fits with their strategic plan to go global, they like the idea that the two most advanced programs are either partnered, or about to be partnered. None of this is personal, just business. Your job is to make the arguments based on logic and put doubt in their minds. Their negotiators are smart and experienced poker players, so they will never let you know they are agreeing with your arguments. Also, keep in mind that at the very end of all this they will be selling their management on all the reasons why this deal should be done and that it is worth much more than a low-ball offer. The schedules you provide them, the ones that make you're your arguments, will be used in the executive office of Buyer A's at some point in some form. Understand that the negotiators have to sell the senior management, and the senior management has to sell the board, and both have to sell the Buyer A shareholders if your acquisition is large enough to require Buyer A's shareholder vote. Some of the arguments on Product A you will make are:

- Launch date:
  - You will show them a more detailed project plan that adds more creditability to your timeline. It would help if some of this came from BigPharma A, but if not, it should be prepared and supported by your executive team responsible for development.
  - You do not anticipate the launch being delayed, period.
  - Your major argument to Buyer A is that the beauty of the royalty stream from Products A and B is that when the huge royalty payments come to Buyer A they will be pure profit, with no costs associated with them, and no effort on the organization as these are then passive profits. The incremental cash flow to Buyer A will either:
    - Offset the higher development costs in later years as they build their global pipeline, or
    - Increase earnings per share and equity value for all shareholders
- Sales Dollar & Units Forecast:
  - The price BigPharma A has assumed is similar to 1-2 other products (show support) and has a superior efficacy and safety profile accepted by all medical insurance carriers. There is not reason to believe the forecasted price is too high as the analysis shows it is more than justified based on the (attached) economic analysis
  - The market penetration rates of Product A are too high and could even be higher. Provide an example of a past product

launch of a similar product and attempt to show the penetration rates of that growth period. The same would apply to other European territories and the growth rates are very clearly reasonable.

- The prices in Europe and Japan already reflect a 25% lower price than the US, (sorry if we did not make that clear)
- Regulatory Approval:
  - Key markets such as Europe and Japan will not follow in 12 months or less just like (show an example of such an approval) because BigPharma A is accelerating the ex-US development and regulatory activities to have all ex-US approvals come as soon as possible. They have the money and human resources to do this and they are doing it.
  - The Other (ROW-rest of world) territory projection same issue as above on timing and the ROW pricing is already 35% lower than the US (sorry we did not make that clear)
- Discount Rate:
  - You will never agree on the discount rate but be prepared to split the difference between a rate you proposed and a rate they really think is reasonable. You might suggest a discount rate of 20%; they might suggest a 40% discount rate. The valuations associated with these two discount rates are very different with a Net Present Value of $90 million at 20%, and an NPV of $28 million at 40%. You will argue this point but let's presume the parties come together at 30% and they set a NPV for Product A at $48 million.
- Buyer A's Common Shares:
  - You will make the argument that there is risk in taking 50% of the deal price in the equity of Buyer A. It could be that Buyer A has had erratic earnings in the past 2-3 years that concern you. Some of your products are getting old, tired and losing share
  - The ABC Biotech Company is well funded today, has a great investor base that is ready and willing to raise more capital from them, and 2-3 investment banking firms that have interest in taking the company public

- ABC management has to be convinced that taking Buyer A's stock is better than keeping our own.
- You know they can't do this, but consider asking for the deal to be done 100% in cash.
- These are good arguments that you can push on your concerns about their shares to the very last discussion. This is one of high-level reasons you do not have to do this deal, and a very good reason they have to sell ABC as to why their deal is better. This is how you use an argument to extract more value, but make sure it is a good, solid, logical argument.
- Maybe the price is $140 million if cash, $175 million if 50% stock. So the arguments continue, and continue.
- Timing:
  - If the ABC Biotech Company chose to delay their exit for two years from now, the NPV calculation for all the various development programs. The Net Present Value calculations will increase. For example, using Table E, if The ABC Biotech company waited two years to do an exit and all other assumptions remained the same the NPV value for Product A at a 30% discount factor would calculate to $81 Million instead of $48 Million. The same concept would theoretically increase the value of Products B through D, plus the preclinical pipeline.
  - Obviously, the above can be a useful argument but also consider that something can go wrong over the next two years to decrease value. So make the argument, but consider the risk involved in waiting another two years.

The point of all this is to illustrate how one might begin to make arguments that are the basis for a complex negotiation program. This will takes weeks/months not days. Each deal is difference so there is no roadmap other than to point out that preparation counts, logical arguments that the other side can respect will be impactful, and what both sides are doing is developing a giant file of information from which to make arguments with up the line to their respective management hierarchy.

Going Further With This Deal.

OK, so let's say you magically agree on a value of $34 million for Product A. Now you have to so something similar with Product B, C, D and the pre-clinical pipeline.

Perhaps after a lot of work similar to the analysis prepared for Product A, you come up with values for the above Products as follows:

$ 25.0 million – Product B
$ 17.5 million – Product C
$ 12.5 million – Product D
$ 5.0 million – entire preclinical pipeline

Program	Fair Estimate of Net Present Value	Comments
Product A	$ 48 million	Already licensed to Big Pharma A
Product B	25 million	In negotiations right now
Product C	17.5 million	Not partnered – wanted by Buyer A
Product D	12.5 million	Not partnered – wanted by Buyer A
Pre-clinical Pipeline	5 million	Not partnered – wanted by Buyer A
Total Net Present Value Of Technology	$ 108 million	

Next let us add other ABC Biotech Assets that will be acquired to include the following:

Asset	Fair Estimate of Net Present Value	Comments
Development Facilities	$13 million	This represents the replacement cost of this facility if one were to build it today at current prices
ABC Biotech Employees (Recruited, relocated, trained and in place working programs)	$ 2 million	You cannot sell the employees obviously, but having a quality team working and in place has timing value and that is the argument
Intellectual Property Estate	$7 million	This represents the additional value of the patent estate that is not currently utilized by active development programs. Your patent estate is broad and can apply to several therapeutic that can be exploited but have not been due to financial constraints
Net Balance Sheet Assets	$10 million	These are hard financial assets such a cash and liquid securities, accounts receivable, less liabilities
Total Net Present Value of Non-Technology Value	$32 million	

Recapping the Hypothetical Net Present Value Analysis of ABC Biotech:

So after weeks/months of discussions, the negotiating parties come up with a an acquisition value of $115 million for the ABC Biotech Company, as follows:

Technology Value	$ 108 million
Other Value – not technology	$ 32 million
Total Acquisition Value	**$ 140 million**

Now to complete the loop, let's refer back to the Capital Formation Table A in Chapter 4. In Charter 4 we determined that reach this current point in development over $30 million in equity would be raised and just under 10.5 million shares would be issued. If the exit deal closes at $140 million, that valuation amounts to $13.33/share. After considering the issuance of stock options granted over time to your executives, board members and advisors at the then valuation of the each offering, the overall average price per share amounts to approximately $12.00/share.

<u>Overall Summary of this Hypothetical Deal:</u>

- A total of $30 million was invested over time and returned $140 million
- The discounted technology NPV of Product A amounted to $48 million. However, it is interesting to note that this valuation was bolstered by an additional three years of patent life that created three more market years worth $12.5 million after discounting. Without this extension of market protection, Product A's NPV would have only been $35.8 million, or about a 9% of the deal payout ($1.00/share) and this was for only one product. The point is that the extension mattered.
- Each shareholder received $12.00 a share after the payout of the stock options to the team. The lead investor paid $1.25/share, and received $12.00/share for a 9.6 fold return on investment.
- The average professional investor paid $3.24/share, and received $12.00 for a 3.7 fold return on capital
- The last professionals that paid the highest prices when the risks were lower paid $5.00/share, and received $12.00 for a 2.4 fold return of capital
- Your executive team, board members, and advisors were recruited over a period of time and received an aggregate total of 1,500,000 stock options with strike prices (the exercise price) averaging $2.88/share. After being cashed out at $12.00 their average profit per share (option share) was $9.12 and they did not put any capital at risk. Approximately $13.7 Million will be paid out to this group that will probably involve 20 people or more.
- Your seed investors received a payout of twelve times their original investment and they took the highest risk.
- Your 1 million founder's shares returned you $12 million and you earned it!

In the end it often boils down to one number. Now there will always be the final macho push for a certain number by each side. One side may say they won't accept any number under $150 million and the other side says they won't pay any more than $130 million. The art of making meaningful, constructive arguments continues. Eventually one party convinces the other party their way, or the party that wants it more softens their position, and the final compromise takes place. As you can see, so much of negotiation is about arguing positions so you can see how all the preparation becomes important fuel for such activities that are necessary to get you to the above final point in the negotiations.

When all deal terms are agreed upon a draft contract is prepared. That contract draft will be the basis for a number of contract language changes that will take place over a period of week until it reaches a point of mutual acceptance. At that acceptance point management on both sides will sign the agreement subject to the approval of their respective boards of directors and shareholders. Once the respective boards and shareholders approve it the contract becomes valid and you will proceed to closing.

Closing will involve a number of formal legal matters and will largely be driven by the attorneys on both sides protecting the interests of their respective clients. The specific issues will always vary depending on the deal but this is a necessary final step and you need to understand that the deal is not over until the closing is finalized.

Other Food for Thought on This Case Study
Instead of a 100% acquisition, ABC Biotech could choose to sell everything except Products A and B, especially if Buyer A is having trouble accepting your proposed valuation. The deal could close as planned with a lower price for all other assets and the royalty streams for Product A and B could be place into a royalty trust for later distribution to the shareholders on a prorate basis of their percent ownership. The argument would then be that if the royalty streams for both programs were high the shareholder would not be taking a discounted value at this time.

The other side of the argument is that a cash bird in the hand is better now and let Buyer A take all the risk. The point is that the use of creative structures in negotiating deals can help to mitigate deal-breaking issues to the satisfaction of both parties and allow the main deal to close. Like everything else in your business much of this comes with experience so use experienced professionals to help you do major transactions like this at all times.

Other Valuation Methods

There are several other valuation methods that we did not cover due to the nature of this kind of a business model. Other methods include a multiple of earnings, a multiple of sales, other comparables sales. These alternative methods are usually difficult to apply to early technology company business models because they lack hard cash flow streams but are an important part of evaluating businesses with reliable future cash flow streams.

Form of the Transaction

The exit transaction could take many forms, and you must remain open to forms that may be different from what you had in mind. Most likely the acquiring party will determine the structure of the transaction that may be beneficial to them, and you will generally try to accommodate them with some adjustments. If you are lucky, you will be able to dictate the structure and terms, subject to reasonable adjustments.

Other Possible Exit Deal Structures

The following are just a few types of common exit transactions you might encounter.

Example 1: An offer to buy 100 percent of the stock in your company in what you would want to be a tax-free exchange transaction. Alternatively, the firm may offer cash, or a combination of cash and stock. This is similar to the above case study illustration.

Example 2: An offer for a worldwide purchase of your products or technologies in the form of a front payment and predetermined periodic ongoing payments, with a final payment in later years. That same structure might involve royalties on sales for a certain period, with or without minimum annual royalties.

Example 3: A joint venture where the other party sequentially takes over all operations, which might have a front payment but be heavily weighted on sales of the products or technology for a period, with or without minimums. The same structure could involve a portion of the third party's stock to reduce their cash requirement and enable you to participate in their commercial success.

Example 4: The spin out of a major asset/technology, leaving the balance of the portfolio in your hands. This remuneration received in this spinout could form the basis of a partial exit in the form of a special dividend, a stock buyback, or some other creative method that allows major shareholders to take some cash off the table while you continue to develop other interesting programs.

The point here is that there are endless structures that can work and that you may encounter during an exit transaction. Being flexible and creative is important because at the end of the day, there are many ways for a third party to contribute value to you in the way of an exit.

Take away issues

- Know the needs, wants and fears of your buyer
- Be optimistic about the value of your company but temper that with the knowledge that a number of major risk factors will present themselves between now and the first royalty payment.
- Negotiate the deal with logical arguments that you have carefully prepared and quantified
- Be prepared to make the final big decision to take the deal or leave it

CHAPTER 13

CONCLUSION

Let's kick back and reflect on this fabulous journey

We completed a long journey from a great idea to a great payoff that I hope you found interesting and informative. As mentioned in the beginning of this book, this business is not for everybody and not everybody can or should be a CEO. Hopefully, the information provided in this book either encourages you to start a Life Science company and be its CEO, or directs you to be key member of a great team instead of the CEO. Either decision works as you can achieve a great deal of satisfaction with either pathway. The point is to be part of something great that you can be proud of, and also be rewarded for it.

In this book I have attempted to speak to you as an advisor. Any start-up Life Sciences Company is exhilaratingly and challenging, it is also all consuming with high risk. Some make it big, others learn from the experience only to do it again, others learn but lose opportunity time.

This book may have provided you some thoughts about whether you have a great idea, or a disruptive idea, and whether or not you should charge with your idea or wait until you can fund the first meaningful intellectual property milestone.

The value of intellectual property and the useful remaining market life of that intellectual property are extremely important. Twenty years from the filing date can go fast with products that can have ten-year gestation cycles. Perhaps this book has convinced you that you need to focus on the useful marketing life of a product as a potential corporate partner views it. Market years equate to royalty years, which equate to annual cash flow, and finally the basis for an exit valuation. Consider optimizing your intellection property program and do all you can within reason to add patents and patent breath and depth to lengthen and strengthen market life.

Fund raising is something that now you may view as an ongoing effort instead of an event. Try not to make the typical rooky mistake of taking the first investor that offers you a deal that continues to allow you to control the company. What you really need is the very best investor group that is highly respected by their peers to be your lead investor. Yes you will have a much lower percent of the company after that first professional funding and you will likely no longer have control, but you will do better in the long run if you have good professional investors.

You as the CEO are the most important factor in fund raising. If the investors like you, and more importantly they believe in you, they will fund you, if not they pass and you will never really know why. Sure, they will mention technology and other concerns, but the real reason is they don't want to invest in you and they will not say that. You will be measured by the strength of your team. The investors will presume that the people you pick for your team represent the highest level of talent you are capable of recruiting. If they are not good enough then it reflects poorly on you. Hopefully, you understand that your Board as well as the broader, collection of advisors your have retained, are also part of you team and the same standard also applies to them.

The culture of your company starts with you. It is not what you say; it is what you do that matters most. Everybody is watching you whether you realize it or not, so understand every moment of every day you are sending non-verbal signals that are being picked up by the people around you. Do your best to make sure those signals are positive and constructive.

As you set goals and objectives for the company make sure you really mean it. There is no reason to hide such important information. Celebrate your goals and communicate them widely. Everybody likes to know where they are heading and it gives the team a reason to take pride in the company and be pleased they are part of the team.

Recruit the best executives you can find, they in term will recruit the best members of their respective teams they can find. You can never have too good a team. Weak managers tend to hire weak staff. Your executive team is one of your most valuable assets and they will enable you to achieve your long-term goals.

Management is not easy but instead is a lot of hard work. How you manage all the resources you have under your control has so much to do with achieving high levels of valuation at the end. With efficient and effective management programs you should have fewer delays and lower cost. This will ultimately result in more market years of royalties and possibly will reduce the level of overall funding needed to achieve you goals. Less funding means less dilution, which then means a higher per share payout at the end.

Your choice of a business model is important in determining how you need to staff and fund such a company. Either model can be very successful and can be very exciting and rewarding. However, each model requires a different compliment of management skill sets at varying levels, so think it through carefully. The more important issue is to recognize the differences, because while either business model will work, they operate in different ways and require different team configurations and skill sets.

When the time comes to build real value, you and your team need to be at the top of your/their game. This is championship game time. It is the phase of the company you have been preparing for and the phase of the company that will put you within arms length of your goals. Do your best to cull and improve your team to keep it a championship quality team at all times. Push the team, stretch each member, enable each member to grow, and you will be surprised how well they perform.

Eventually you will have the pleasure of soliciting prospective partners and receiving calls from interest prospective partners. Remember you only get one change to make a first impression. Make it work with the right package and the right team. Always remember that while you may have some great technology, the other side is going to take on the very large financial risk and they worry that something you did along the way may hurt them in front of the FDA at some point in time. Give them the confidence that you know what they have to deal with, you are a committed and responsible partner, and that you have their best interests in mind at all times. You only succeed if they do, so their success is your only way of succeeding.

Negotiate deals fairly and reasonably. Be enthusiastic about your technology but always remember that there is a great deal of risk in your business that you are expecting the other party to take. Sometimes you may start to believe your technology or products are more valuable than they really are. When you start to believe you own PR talking points are indisputably correct and certain this would indicate the point at which you need a reality check. Accept deals with reasonable valuations and you will be happy in the long run. There are large graveyards that are the resting place for development programs that used to be great before they advanced to the next phase and developed a safety problem or a new technical challenge. Your business requires a high degree of skill, but it also takes a fair amount of luck so remain realistic and flexible at all times.

When you close your final deal, make sure you profusely thank all of your team that is your executives, the staff, the advisors and your board. Remember it was this fantastic team that brought you to the goal line.

Chances are this may not be the last deal you do. Much of what you learn from this experience can be used again. Now, after doing one start-up you know what to expect, and perhaps the next time you will make fewer mistakes, and take advantage of more opportunities, and make better early decisions on important matters. Mistakes are good because they teach you important lessons, and the more mistakes you make the better CEO you will become.

I am excited for you on taking this venture. There is nothing more fun, more motivating, more challenging, and more all consuming, than starting up a company and taking it through an exit. I hope this one is fun and rewarding for you and allows you to achieve something you can be very, very proud of and do some good for others. If this book has helped in some very small way you will have made me proud.

ACKNOWLEDGMENTS

I wish to thank my family for putting up with me all these years as I moved from one job to another, and one company to another, all involving a great deal of time away from home. My family's ability to support me enabled me to do what I did, and for that I will always be grateful to my wife and daughters.

Thank you to the many exceptionally great bosses, advisors, employees, and coworkers that I was privileged to serve. They guided me, challenged me, taught me, allowed me to learn and participate, and offered me the opportunity to improve over the years and take on increasing responsibilities. Collectively they taught me what I know, and I am forever indebted to them for all their help and support.

It is my hope that the material in this book will provide you a certain level of guidance and, in a sense, an emotional compass on how to manage your decision process in an objective manner. If this book can help you develop a better pathway, or avoid mistakes, or stay focused on all the right things from the start, then I have achieved my purpose. It is like building a house with a strong foundation instead of a weak foundation. Do it right the first time, and you will be glad you did.

Your comments about this book are greatly appreciated. Should you wish to discuss my consulting or board of director services in more detail, please correspond with me at jjluchese@gmail.com.